Date D

W/D

ENDING IN EARNEST

ENDING IN EARNEST

A Literary Log by

REBECCA WEST

Essay Index Reprint Series

BOOKS FOR LIBRARIES PRESS, INC.
FREEPORT, NEW YORK

First published 1931
Reprinted 1967

TO

EMANIE SACHS

FOREWORD

THESE notes represent most of the material which I contributed to the *Bookman* during 1929 and 1930, as "Letters from Europe," with a few alterations and additions suggested to me by correspondents. The personal manner in which they are written must not be regarded as a sign of undue egotism on my part, but as a result of the agreement between myself and the editor that this was the most useful form they could take at the time; and their episodic nature is due to that cause also.

REBECCA WEST

CONTENTS

ix

CONTENTS

ENDING IN EARNEST

RESCUED
FROM EXCESS

So MANY books are published nowadays that works deserving of a considerable measure of survival are swamped almost immediately and sink into the region of the forgotten. It shocked me to see that when Arnold Rothstein was shot and the newspapers were publishing all the information about him they could find, not one journalist mentioned that he had obviously served Mr. Scott Fitzgerald as model for Meyer Wolfsheim in *The Great Gatsby*. Yet *The Great Gatsby* was surely a remarkable novel. For one thing it gave a superbly imaginative vision of the gaunt outskirts of New York, where the same force that makes the city sends up sporadic buildings, but does not form them or the life they house into civilized patterns as it does in the city. The prodigiousness of the garage proprietor and his wife, and their complete irrelevance to anything but violence, linger in my mind as vividly as when I read it; and so does the damnation of Daisy and her husband and her friends when they drift into this world of violence because they are incapable of doing anything in their own. This novel has not been superseded in the common mind by better books: merely by other books.

Bad as this excess of publication is when it steals from us the memory of what we have read, it is worse still when it prevents us even finding out what we should enjoy reading. I have no time to read the French reviews regularly, and so it was only by the good luck of reading an article in the *New Statesman*, by Mr. T. W. Earp, the art critic, that I discovered that an extremely interesting book on Claude Monet has just been published by, of all people in the world, M. Clemenceau. They were apparently great friends, and indeed Monet's great healthy body would make him feel amity for "The Tiger," who, whatever else he may be, is certainly a good animal. The particular phase of Monet's being treated by Clemenceau in this little book is that which resulted in *Les Nymphéas:* the series of paintings in which he rendered various aspects of his water gardens. We have one panel in London in the Tate Gallery: which has some very lovely modern French painting. But most of them are in the singularly bashful Musée de l'Orangerie, a sister-ship to the Jeu du Paume building, in the Jardin des Tuileries, but over on the Seine side

where nobody sees it. It would be worth visiting if
only to see the beautiful recumbent figure just outside it which is Maillol's Memorial to Cézanne;
but it is the Monets inside which make a visit to it
one of the best experiences the world has to offer.
Bourgeois art, if you insist; but nobody objects to
that except members of the bourgeoisie trying to
escape from themselves.

One goes into two rooms, each wall of which is
covered by a long low picture of some part of a
water garden, including in each case some water
lilies, and finds that these eight panels, which form a
factual point of view, are thematically monotonous,
are all completely different, and all of the first
importance in the emotions they create. There is
one in particular that most beautifully presents the
static and the dynamic in relation. At the bottom of
the canvas are the firm nodes of four or five water
lilies on which the whole composition seems to be
resting. Light fused with the colour of sky and cloud
is reflected from all over the sunlit water with the
extremest vivacity; and willow branches droop
down through this pattern, superimposing on it
another pattern of a rhythm different but in divine
agreement. The result of this balance is the most
beautiful sense of serenity which one cannot help
projecting upon the painter. One finds oneself
thinking that when Monet painted these pictures
he must have arrived at a state of complete happi-

ness, have gone to stay with someone kind and wealthy who treated him like a beloved child and had had those lily ponds ready for him in the garden; when he was encouraged to spend long days contemplating them in perfect tranquillity, while silent servants took out thoughtfully ordered little meals on trays.

But M. Clemenceau's book tells us that in fact these lily ponds were in Monet's own garden, through which there ran an automobile highway and a railroad track; and he had to make them himself before he started in to paint them. Moreover, during the decade he worked on them he was perpetually harassed by eye trouble and operations. It is a curious example of what a vast gulf often divides a work of art and the external experience of the artist. There was, as it turns out, no simple ingredient in the process that led to *Les Nymphéas*. For even the lily ponds were not the simple stimuli that might be supposed. The other day at the Lefevre Galleries here in London I was shown a very beautiful Cézanne, which represented flowers in a garden urn, girt in shadow by the tall rounded stonework of a fountain, that in its turn was girt in sunlight by the tall rounded firmament of a shadeless summer day. It was a curiously uncharacteristic Cézanne, and I said, "That picture reminds me more of Monet's *Les Nymphéas* than any other picture I have ever seen." It turned out that Monet had owned it. His lily ponds were merely called in as part of a silent discussion between the two great painters' minds regarding the possibility of rendering certain sorts of visual experiences.

W<small>HEN</small> Plymouth Harbour spun round the *Maure-*
tania, as harbours do round ships that have to keep
their footing on the tides while they kiss the mails
good-bye and tell the tender how well it is looking,
England looked a green and innocent land. This
West Country landscape might well be part of the
dreams of "The Brushwood Boy." But on the contrary, as one might say, England proved to be pre-
occupied with the consignment of *The Well of*
Loneliness to the furnaces of Scotland Yard as an
obscene book. One wishes it had not, for these proceedings form an imbroglio in which nobody can
play a comfortable part.

The initial complication is that the author, Miss
Radclyffe Hall, is a personality whom most of us
like and admire. She has a kind of austere, work-
manly handsomeness which makes one think of a
very beautifully made sporting rifle or golf club,

6

and though I myself know her but slightly—I have met her perhaps half a dozen times and once dined at her house—I have seen enough of her to realize that her character matches her appearance. She has all the virtues of the English aristocratic type, courage, self-restraint, steadfastness, and a very fine intelligence which—and here she is very typical of her kind, for England is full of old admirals and generals and squires who use their leisure in solving the problem of perpetual motion or foretelling the date of the next war from the measurements of pyramids—likes to exercise itself on eccentric material: she has devised as cunning tests for the spiritualist medium as any researcher alive. This much I know of Miss Radclyffe Hall first hand, and chance has more than once supplemented this knowledge by sending my way information of large and disinterested kindness that she has shown to people in need. The remark of George II that if Wolfe was mad he wished he would bite the other generals might appositely be mentioned here.

Now, that the community should throw contempt on a person like this, who is obviously not contemptible, is of course a dangerous darkening of counsel. Everybody who knows Miss Radclyffe Hall wants to stand by her. But they are finding it far from easy to stand by *The Well of Loneliness*, for the simple reason that it is, in a way which is particularly inconvenient in the present circumstances, not

a very good book. The first part is factually interesting; the second part is far below the standard the
author has set for herself in her other books. A
novel which ends a chapter with the sentence "And
that night they were not divided" cannot redeem
itself by having "they" mean not what it usually
does. Now, no one believes that a book ought to be
suppressed because it is badly written; but it unfortunately happens that the qualities which make
this book a poor one are precisely these that have
been used dialectically in tussles with the censorship
over other books.

When a book of great literary merit is denounced
the first line of defence always is to point out that
that kind of book, which conscientiously analyzes
a human experience and gives its findings honestly,
cannot do those who read it any harm, since it adds
to the knowledge of reality by which man lives. It
has always been emphasized that far more harmful
are books written sentimentally, that is to say written by persons who do not pass their subject matter
through their imaginations and report on the results, but who describe their subject matter without investigation in terms they think likely to cause
certain emotions in their readers. It is to that last
category that *The Well of Loneliness* unhappily belongs. Miss Radclyffe Hall's aim in writing was not
to find out the inner truth of the lives of Stephen
and Mary; it was to excite in the readers certain

friendly emotions toward the lives of Stephen and Mary. The book constantly gives us a sense of fictitious values, of "Cry, damn you, cry," hokum. Hence considerable dismay is being felt by those who are compelled by their belief in a free press to wrestle with the authorities over the suppression of this book, but who realize perfectly well that this is the kind of book they have denounced again and again in the course of other tussles with the censorship.

This accounts for the curious muted tone of the controversy. The situation is not calculated to provoke the impulsive speech that hits the mark. Nobody cares to say, "I think this is a remarkably poor book but I am against its suppression on general principles," because that would be to give the enemy ammunition for their attack on a personality whom one does not wish attacked. But that suppressed reservation takes all the ginger out of the defenses which come to utterance. Hence the round robin of writers protesting against the censoring of the book contained no statement which matched in impressiveness the list of signatories, which included practically every writer of standing, some of them high in academic respectability. But there can be no doubt that if the censorship issue is raised on a book of more distinguished quality during the next year or so there will be an explosion that will raise the roof. For the incident has proved to the hilt the

imbecility of Comstockery. It has exhibited again
its inevitable disposition to magnify the evil that it
pretends to abolish, by raising a scandal.

As a fiction reviewer of long experience I know
that the life of *The Well of Loneliness* would not have
extended beyond four months. By that time it would
have vanished completely from the shelves of the
Times Book Club and the hearts of the people.
Nor, during that time, could it conceivably have
done what the narrowest mind could have considered much harm. It would have been read
chiefly by wondering adults, most of them above
the age when conversion is likely. Its effect on the
young might have been bad, for a priggish adolescent might have had its first emotional stirrings
clarified and sanctified and therefore fixed by those
pages. But such children are unlikely to come into
possession of a high-priced novel which their parents would be reluctant to give them; and the
sophisticated adolescent who has a way of coming
into possession of everything it wants would hardly
enjoy anything so like the earnest novels Miss
Elizabeth Robins wrote in the 'nineties. I would be
willing to bet my entire life ration of caviare and
Berncastler that had *The Well of Loneliness* not been
suppressed it would have made but little dint on
the Day of Judgment.

Now the case is altered. *Time and Tide*, a weekly
journal largely written and read by women, pub-

lished an irritated letter from "A Modern Mother" who tells that she had read *The Well of Loneliness* when it first came out and decided that she preferred her fifteen-year-old daughter not to read a recommendation of homosexuality, and that she had been able to see that the book came into the house and went out of it without her daughter knowing. Since then, however, the book has been censored. In consequence, the newspapers have every day over a long period of time shown placards and published articles which have thrust on every child who can read full knowledge of the existence of female homosexuality, and a newspaper costs a penny, whereas the book cost fifteen shillings. This is a very serious charge against the authorities: particularly when one considers the tendency of wholesome youth to side with the rebel. The imprisonment of Oscar Wilde was the best propaganda that was ever put in for male homosexuality, and now that the government has supplied female homosexuality with a handsome, noble, and intrepid martyr the word Lesbian will in no time suggest to the young girl something other than the friend of Catullus who had bad luck with a sparrow.

The only protection of the community is that England has elected to take the case with laughter. In a burlesque dramatization of *Uncle Tom's Cabin* that is running here just now, Gracie Fields, the comedian who plays Topsy, has altered that patch of dialogue where she professes ignorance of her father and mother and specks she growed. Simply she lifts the confusion onto another plane by naming as her sole progenitor Radclyffe Hall; and the house rocks. Odd the queer things with which Harriet Beecher Stowe gets herself involved: the Civil War, the Byron controversy, *The Well of Loneliness*.

ANOTHER
KIND OF CENSORSHIP

EVER since I came to New York Claudine, pale,
slender, physically and mentally serious, obviously
not the Claudine of whom Colette Willy has written,
has come in once a week throughout my visit to
wash and mend my clothes. We have talked but
little. On the whole she has restricted herself to the
exhortations, characteristic of her nation, towards
an economy which is purely ideal. There is actually
no place in New York where I could have bought
stockings for so much less than I actually paid for
them as she alleges. She has invented it as a myth to
inspire herself and all other female consumers just
as the Syndicalists created the General Strike to
inspire the working classes. Never has she strayed
beyond the confines of this subject and told me her
views on life until the other day, when she was
packing my trunk for my return journey across the
Atlantic. She was concerned lest a picture should

have its glass broken during transit. I said, "Don't bother about that, I am going to put it in another frame, and as they invariably crack the glass when they are taking off this type of frame I don't mind if it gets cracked on the journey." She had been bending over the trunk, but she straightened herself, and faced me as if she were saying something important. "Then it won't get cracked. If you don't care whether it gets cracked or not, it won't get cracked. If you cared, then it would get cracked." She bent over the trunk again, but in a second raised her head and came back to it. "When you get to the other side you must write and tell me if it isn't so. Because you don't care it won't be cracked." Then she returned to her task and a reticence which I do not expect she will abandon again.

It interested me that I could think of no word that comes anywhere near expressing this attitude of mind. It is not pessimism, for that contains no suggestion of animism: and here it is felt that something in the nature of things was either noting one's indifference to the object before ironically giving one the undesired present of its safety, or was moved to destroy it by having nosed out one's attachment to it. We all fall into this way of thinking at times; and when we are children we are sometimes given over to it for days at a time. It seems strange, therefore, that there should not be a word denoting it in quite common use. Probably the implied suspicion that the universe is controlled by a spirit hostile to man is so unwelcome to him that he pushes it away from him as far as possible and will not give it as much anchorage in life as lies in a word. In fact, the instinct for censorship of the subversive works not only on literature but on language.

As it happened, we ate our Christmas dinner at the Cabassud which lies beside the two lakes at Ville d'Avray that Corot was forever painting. It is the inn to which Sapho took her young lover, or to which her young lover took her—have it your own way; and Balzac's villa is just over the road. Before dinner we walked round the lakes, on which floated stars and lamplit windows, and the poplars which were so like each other that they seemed to have reflections beside them as well as in the water beneath them. We went through the woods, gray as a Persian cat now with the moonlight, up to the old coach road from Paris to Versailles. (The road one goes by now was made by Napoleon.) In one of the circles which were cut in the woods every few hundred metres so that the coaches might pass, we stood and named the famous men who had driven that way and soon stopped for lack of breath.

Someone wondered, "Has any country ever had such a prolonged Golden Age as France?" And someone else said, "Why was it that just then so many great men were born?" A third said, "Is a Golden Age an age in which many great men are born, or an age that permits the average man to be as great as he can?" We debated this till fear that the dinner might be spoiled drove us back again to the inn; where one of us picked up a *Continental Daily Mail* and saw that Mona Tattersall and Stacy Aumonier were dead.

Both these calamities had some relevancy to the discussion. Mona Tattersall was a girl in her middle twenties who had in her time left her mark on literature, though literature had left little mark on her. For it was largely the life she and her friends had led round and about the Embassy Club in London, the Potinière at Deauville, and the Sporting Club at Monte Carlo, which made Michael Arlen write *The Green Hat* and other people read it. Her father was a man of great wealth, and she lived with that splendid calm grossness of expenditure that one could imagine in a daughter of the Venetian Republic in its great days. She had that golden fairness which lends glamour to every act and aspect of those who possess it. She had the tireless health which usually comes of simple living in the country, so that when one saw her rosy and jolly as a milkmaid at five in the morning after a twenty-four-hour day spent golfing, swimming, riding, gambling, dancing, dining, one felt that this was a goddess exempt from human limitations. Naturally many people who were not in her set wished that they were. Because of the psychic emptiness of England during the exhausted years following the war, it accepted novels and plays that were based on nothing more important than this wish; though these were plainly as far away from imaginative literature as a manicurist's dream of marrying a millionaire is from creative vision. To-day Michael Arlen is no longer the vogue; where Noel Coward shows the influence of this period he seems old-fashioned; and Frederick Lonsdale, because of his profound sympathy with it, cancels the effect of his own wit. It is eerie that the girl herself should hardly have survived the fashion she engendered. Eerie too that an age, by asking too much of its children, should see that gold should be out of the question and nothing better than gilt be had for years and years.

Yes, if an age would deal fairly well with its children and let them do what they can! Or better still if their frail constitutions were not so unequal to their tasks! That is what the death of Stacy Aumonier made one feel. That charming little human mole with brown eyes and thick fur-like hair and hands that he carried in front of him like paws, might have been an extremely distinguished artist in at least three ways—for he was a delightful painter, a writer with a most tender sense of character, and an impersonator who had excelled Ruth Draper long before she had visited these shores- -if during the last twenty years or so since he had grown up he had ever felt quite well. I suppose he went out of the world without having displayed more than a quarter of his gifts, except benevolence, of which I cannot believe he had much more than he showed, for no human being could have that. One had a bitter sense of waste when one read how tuberculosis had taken him at last up in Switzerland. That same feeling came back to one later in the evening, when one remembered, because we were singing French nursery rhymes, how Elinor Wylie had loved to sing at parties, raising her voice happily, caring no more for its shrillness than a child marching round a Christmas tree whether the trumpet that it blows is cracked.

Elinor Wylie had been in England a good deal during the last few years, and she was always at her best when she was here, perhaps because our sedative airs are more wholesome for those who suffer from high blood pressure than the bracing American climate. She was at once gayer and calmer. Her beauty seemed more a part and expression of herself, and less a hollow statue into which her spirit had fled to take refuge from the innumerable torments raised up against her by her excessive sensibility. At a party given by Robert and Sylvia

Lynd at their house in Hampstead, her face was not
only unlined, it was rounded like a child's, because
she was so pleased at her new dress, a model she
had been able to buy cheaply in Paris, being as
slim as the slim mannequin for whom it had been
made; at the new shoes which revealed the narrow-
ness of her feet, and the new stockings which revealed the shapeliness of her legs; at the week-end
she had just spent among admiring people at a
lovely house in Wiltshire; at the leafy garden where
she was sitting at the moment; at the good time she
was having. Only once during the evening did there
come into her voice that sharpness which showed
that she was at odds with her environment; and because of its reason I find that outburst wholly delightful to remember. Somebody had said that
Edna St. Vincent Millay was obviously finished, it
was so long since she had published a book. So
Elinor was crying out that Edna St. Vincent Millay
was a genius and could not be finished: that there
would come a book quite soon, and that when it
came it would be wonderful, wonderful, wonderful.

But this summer it was plain that England had no
curative magic for her. The last time I saw her was
at a cocktail party given by our gifted Stephen
Tennant in his very beautiful bedroom in his
mother's house in old Westminster. She hobbled
in, still maimed and twisted from her fall down a
flight of stairs. Though weeks had elapsed since it

happened, her face was still that greenish-white colour which people turn when they have just sprained a limb. It had been arranged by the host that she was to lie on the bed, and the party was to gather round her. But when she saw me she limped over to me until she had asked if I had seen the suggestions in the American papers that her fall had been an attempt at suicide. I answered that I had seen them but had not believed them. This, indeed, was the truth; for I had known that at the time she was in unusually good spirits, had heard accounts of her fall from people who had been staying in the house where it happened, and moreover was aware that such a manner of suicide is unheard of outside jail. Tears came into her eyes, and she burst out that that story had been horrible for her husband, as it certainly must have been. One perceived again, as one had so often done when she was sad and indignant, that she had believed everything which had been said to her when she was a débutante. People then had assured her that because she was beautiful and a woman they would worship her endlessly and protect her from all harm; and when they did nothing of the sort and published vile stories about her in the newspapers, she was as hurt as a child who has found itself cheated by an adult.

After that she lay down on the wide bed, which was covered with a cloth-of-silver counterpane, and rested her head on a silver pillow. Her face looked quite gray. But in a little she struggled to her feet again, because our host had handed round brushes and Indian ink and was making us paint our signatures on his lacquered silver walls, and the idea amused and excited her. She made her way round the room, to see what the rest of us had done before she began her effort. There was one signature which she greatly admired, and she clung to the wall below it, looking up wistfully and crying, "Oh, that is beautiful! I shan't be able to do it half so well!" The terrible and absurd despair in her voice was so intense that it staggered one. "How is it possible," one asked oneself, "that a woman who feels little things as acutely as that can go on living for a week?" One also wondered how much in her that struck the superficial observer as egotism was an unbridled passion for perfection too thoroughgoing to exempt herself from praise or blame. It is tragic to realize how often that passion must have been cheated of finding satisfaction in her own work by her treacherous body, which reacted to excitement with an extravagance utterly destructive to the calm of her spirit; and by that still more treacherous part of her spirit which plotted against her by perpetually drawing her within the sphere of excitements. I do not believe we have left to us a tithe of the beauty Elinor Wylie might have created had she been permitted by her own constitution to know peace.

Ｈow do they do it, those artists who have sufficient
sensibility to make their perceptions worth recording and yet protect themselves from receiving any
shocks from their own sensibility, so that they can
keep a steady hand and make a clear record of those
perceptions? I asked myself that question a little
while ago when I went with a friend to one of a
limited number of performances of *La Dame aux
Camélias* which were being given at the Théâtre
Sarah-Bernhardt by the beautiful and brilliant
young French actress, Falconetti. She has more than
the ordinary measure of importance. She looks as
Lina Cavalieri must have looked in her youth;
and in the stylized film, *The Passion of St. Joan,* in
which she played the saint, she dissembled that
beauty by cropping her hair and assuming a sturdy
peasant face, and showed herself able to get her
effect by something very near genius. It was this

23

film, by the way, that drew from the ecclesiastical
authorities a most singular tribute to her powers.
They successfully appealed to the censor for the
deletion of a certain scene in which Falconetti
depicted the effects on Joan of the judge's demand
that she should choose between the sacrament and
her voices, on the ground that it was provocative of
anti-clerical passion. Yet that scene consists of nothing but a close-up of her hands covering her face.

This is plainly no negligible actress. But in *La
Dame aux Camélias* she was played right off the stage
by someone else. I found myself crying, and turned
to my companion and said, "I hope you don't
think I'm crying over Falconetti's performance.
I'm crying over the performance of Sarah Bernhardt, whom I saw in this part twenty-five years
ago, when I was a child of ten. I can remember
every movement and inflection of hers as this
woman speaks the lines." And she answered,
"Don't you see I'm crying too? And it's for the
same reason. But it's longer still since I saw her. It
must be twenty-seven years ago." The dead walked
on the stage so substantially that as we left the
theatre we were agreeing with each other, just as if
we were commenting on a contemporary performance, that the last generation talked the stark-
est and silliest nonsense when it said that Sarah
Bernhardt never played any character but herself.
Her Marguerite Gautier was an exquisitely con-

sistent creation. It was full of touches that built up the character of a woman who accepted all the moral conventions of her world and yet slipped into the place of contempt it reserved for cocottes. In the death scene, when the doctor came in, one could see her drawing on her last reserves of energy, to sit up, to be beautiful for him, to flirt a little with him out of something almost identical with the child's desire to climb onto the knees of the adults that are good to it and wind its arms round their necks, causing kindness, perpetuating it, returning it. When she told him that two of her friends were getting married and said wistfully, "It seems that it is only me who is not going to be happy," she said it interrogatively, as if she thought it possible that he might give her an explanation of her ravaged destiny which would show it as an integral and necessary part of the universe, and that if she could hear it she would no longer rebel against the suffering. Thus did she convey the amiability and the supineness of the naïve cocotte who will submit to innumerable embraces, each time in the childish faith that they are going to develop into a relationship full of love and tenderness, and who will not revolt against being pushed into a position where the world miscalls her, out of the childish feeling that somehow adults have a right to punish her. And she had been building up this impression throughout the whole play, notably in that scene

with Armand Duval's father, where she puts up so
little fight against society's view that she is a dangerous associate and so plainly agrees that if anybody
is going to suffer it might as well be herself. Pure
emotionalism indeed! Henry James had not a nicer
sense of how to construct a unity out of minute
psychological touches.

To leave such a deep impression after a quarter of
a century, a performance must have been as clear
and definite as the most finely cut intaglio. And
who cut this intaglio? Who but the worn and febrile
Sarah, the banner of her being tattered by her
forty years of theatre; by her revolt against the
squalor of her early circumstances; by her unnecessary fight against the drugs which she so
loathed and feared, but which were far dearer than
herself to those who were most dear to her; by
innumerable hurts inflicted by lover and child!
How did she do it? The only explanation that seems
to answer is that she did it because she was French
and had therefore an overwhelming sense of the importance of doing her job. She felt that whatever
happened she had to go on acting, and acting as
well as she knew how, just as most French cooks
consider themselves under an obligation to cook
as well as they know how. Avaricious and so far as
her conscious judgment was concerned utterly
contemptuous of æsthetic values, she was safely

tethered to art by a national characteristic which
has nothing in particular to do with the arts.

The most extreme example of it that I ever came
across, indeed, was far outside the artistic sphere.
I once rented a house in the department of Var,
with a pleasant garden which was efficiently tended
by a repellent part-time gardener, a rude man, not
nice to his wife or cleanly in his appearance. It
afforded me great satisfaction that I was not paying
his wages, as my lease left that duty to the landlord;
until one day inquiry as to why he was working
either preposterously early or preposterously late
elicited the fact that this arrangement meant that
he was getting no wages at all, since the landlord
was a happy bankrupt in whose universe the idea
of paying anybody anything had no place. Simply
he was working for nothing. When asked why he
was doing this, he explained that as he had made the
garden when the house was built it was not in him
to let it go to rack and ruin; so he tended it before
and after having done a whole day's work elsewhere. I do not wish to paint too idyllic a picture
of the situation. Being a Frenchman, he loved
money and reacted to his consciousness that he was
working for none by behaving with the most un-
endearing dourness. But all the same, he did the
work.

Nor do I want to paint the general situation too

idyllically, either. This sense of the importance of doing one's job well is, like all national characteristics, not universally operative in the citizen of that nation; and where it is lacking one plumbs unimaginable depths of incapacity. If a Frenchman does not do his job supremely well he does it almost as badly as is possible for a child of man. Hence a foreigner's life in France is spent in alternate rages at subhuman inefficiency and exaltations at superhuman efficiency. But though this factor is not universally operative it is powerful enough to give it a claim to be in part responsible for the vast contributions France has made to art. How great that part may be can be judged if one contrasts the careers of Bernhardt and Duse. Bernhardt had as many miseries in her life as Duse; but she went on working. She played continuously, and she played everywhere. Practically everybody I know who is older than myself saw her several times, practically everybody I know who is of my generation saw her at least once. I saw her four times before I was sixteen, and I lived in Edinburgh. Through this constant exercise of her art she achieved discipline in the matter concerning which it is most difficult for actresses to practise control: her impersonations were true impersonations, uncoloured by her personal desire to strike her audiences as any particular sort of woman. Duse did not go on working. My generation, and the one before it, could judge her only by a few performances she gave in London the year she died; and by then her art, rusty with disuse, had lost its integrity. She turned every character she played into an apology for suffering, a glorification of the masochism which had shaped her private life.

COMPARE the movement in France which ran parallel to *The Green Hat* movement in England. I have no great admiration for the excessively contemporary muse of Monsieur Paul Morand, who wears on his countenance an unbecoming air of dread that he has missed some social or literary bus which a prudent young French novelist ought to have caught; and it is surely only by chance that Monsieur Jean Giraudoux (author of the amusing *Bella*, which the Knopfs published in translation) became a writer instead of a designer of smart luggage, or of that awful French modernist furniture which exists to show that Euclid too can be common. But it must be admitted that they never forgot the importance of doing their jobs well. Always they paid respect to literary decorum. When England wanted to hear pretty stories about wonderful golden Miss Mammons who could dance all night without getting tired, and practise all the other recreations with equal indefatigability and evasion of their consequences, it did not care what happened to the art of the novel so long as it got its wish-fulfilment phantasies. But France insisted that those who gave it its pipe dreams should not violate literary standards. Hence, though France cannot boast of such an effluescence as England has seen during the last twelve months—there is nothing in the Paris bookshops to compare with London's amazing yield, Virginia Woolf's *Orlando*, Siegfried Sassoon's *Memoirs of a Fox-hunting Man*, and Lytton Strachey's *Elizabeth and Essex*—it can at least say that it never fell so low as England in the years immediately following the war. Those years for us were lost, so far as literature is concerned, except for a few isolated books, written out of a powerful preoccupation, such as Walter de la Mare's *Memoirs of a Midget* and E. M. Forster's *A Passage to India*—and the works of writers such as James Joyce and Lawrence, who had shaken the dust of England off their feet.

This same sense of the importance of the job which prevents French readers and writers losing their standards in times of historic pressure makes the individual artist a more dogged performer than his English or American prototype. Particularly is this observable in the case of women writers. It is impossible to calculate how long or how often Colette Willy would have had to abstain from writing had she taken as a pattern Jane Austen's abstention from literature for seven years as a result of a broken engagement. Instead, she has produced a long shelf of volumes, of which a very fair proportion are little masterpieces.

I LIVE two miles or so from Piccadilly Circus, in an apartment carved out of a mid-Victorian mansion, just over the way from the house where Thackeray was living when he started the *Cornhill Magazine*. It is unbeautiful, being given the colour of a hippopotamus by stucco and gray brick, and the ungainliness of a hippopotamus by a thoroughly bad design. One lives there only because there is a green plenitude of communal gardens all about it. In summer I sit and work on a wide balcony under the dancing shade of a poplar and look down on a lawn fringed by the best of whatever the month brings in flowers, which is the common pleasance of the block; and during my five minutes' walk to the nearest taxi rank and subway station I pass four squares, which are every one of them sylvan glades. This is due to the extreme æsthetic sensibility of Queen Victoria's Consort, Prince Albert. This

33

district was developed by the Great Exhibition of
1857, which was held in an adjacent part of Hyde
Park, and Prince Albert supervised the plans. To
this task he brought the intense love of beauty
which, working in the sphere of nature, made him
devise the afforestation schemes responsible for some
of the loveliest woodland scenery in England, and
which, working in the sphere of art, made him do
much for music in this country. It is ironical to consider that probably no historical character is more
closely identified with sheer bad taste than poor
Prince Albert, for no other reason than that his
widow erected the hideous Albert Hall and Albert
Memorial in his honour. This universe is not entirely just.

I meditated on his wrongs this afternoon, as I
walked along Piccadilly, which I followed to a
point some way past the Albany. That, as you
know, is the rambling collection of bachelors'
apartments in which Byron lived; it was formerly
the town house of the Melbournes. Then I turned
down an alley by St. James's Church, which was
built by Wren, and made my way to the London
Library, which was founded as a result of Thomas
Carlyle's incapacity to buy some books he needed
for his work. Throughout that walk I believe I
thought of nobody who belonged to an age later
than Albert the Good. Why should I? I pass no
buildings which are not either old or designed to

harmonize with old neighbours. Not one single architect has found it possible to erect anywhere in those two miles a façade that has any reference to modern life. Moreover, I passed buildings without number which recall my childhood. Very easily can I imagine that I have shrunken to a trifle under four feet and am trotting along beside the tall ghosts of my father and my uncle, who gossip with moustached lips of Chamberlain, Balfour, Rhodes, Salisbury, and dead Gladstone; and who sometimes point at great houses the canes (without which their generation could not walk) and speak of Palmerston, Disraeli, Peel, the Iron Duke, and other names belonging to an antiquity so much remoter than themselves that one knew that they were going back to the past, and felt themselves as trotting children beside tall ghosts. In fact, when I am not feeling in a mood to stand up manfully to life, London enables me to pass in the drooping of an eyelid to a comfortable revisiting of the past; and I can disregard, and dislike for their invasions on my reverie, the people in the streets who happen to compose the age in which I live.

It is because every moderately intelligent and literate person who lives in London (or indeed in any part of England) is perpetually exposed to this fourth dimensional temptation that there has arisen a particularly scandalous state of affairs in modern English criticism. Recently I was obliged to flee

to a hotel by the circumstance that the frozen pipes
of my apartment had burst and flooded the base-
ment, in consequence of which I was left without
water or gas or electric light. (There is no department of life in which our contact with the past is
more direct than in our domestic architecture.)
Wearied by struggles with insubordinate nature, at
an early hour in the evening I disposed my dog in his
basket with a marrow bone and myself in bed with
two highly praised novels, and hoped we would
be on an equal plane of satisfaction. Believe me,
we were not. Both novels were twaddle, flat, plain
twaddle, immediately recognizable as such by
persons of normal sight. The first was a novel pur-
porting to give an account of the life of a vivandière
with Napoleon's armies during the Russian campaign. Surprise has been expressed by many because its author is quite a young woman; yet such
surprise as is justly adherent to the work springs
from the circumstance that it was written by any
other than a schoolgirl of sixteen, seduced into
authorship by the glossy pages and marbled covers
of a new exercise book rather than by any specific literary bent. It is as mawkish and missish as
could be. One is left with the impression that
Napoleon's soldiers would have fled from a representative group of Miss Spencer's pupils as from
a tough crowd. The prettification of life characteristic of the author's vision can be judged from an

incident in which two beautiful Russian girls are found frozen to death in a carriage crossing the plains and are represented as being exquisite with the supernatural glow of waxen fruit under glass, with the intensified perfection of branches picked out with frost. Not in the universe of this book are the green and violet pallors of those killed by cold, their pitiful lumpishness, or any other horrors. They are excluded not as a result of a selective process. Simply it is that the whole of reality is barred from those pages; so there is no truth or beauty either. Yet this was a better book than the other, which was the stodgiest conceivable compilation of insignificant adventures, a little sister to a bread poultice. This review of the heroine is a fair sample:

"It is indeed a nice point," she remembered reading, "to decide which of the two is the greater, the man who thinks of the way in which to do things or the man who does them; but we may safely conclude that the inventor and the exploiter are necessary to each other, since the one without the other would be useless." Was that not true, too, of herself and Annice, and of the myriads in the world who fell into rank behind them? Annice, indeed, had lived and exploited life to the full, but it was Lydia who had made it possible for her to do so. If it was good that there should be life and love—and Lydia felt that it was good—then those who made such life possible were not without their value, spinsterish, dull and duty-ridden though they might seem. And at this their favourite platitude—"it takes all sorts to make a world"—beat upon

Lydia's mind with new force. It did, indeed, take all sorts to *make* a world; Annice and she between them had *made* Annice's rich and exciting life, had made possible the younger generation clustering about Annice's life, and in the handing of it on to the next generation there was a kind of common achievement, a partnership between them.

Is this one of the Elsie Dinsmore books? No, of course it isn't! The Elsie Dinsmore books are far more sophisticated.

Now, why did these books enjoy the passionate favour of the English critics?—who, I take my oath, have given these insipidities concerning the vivandière as good reviews as anything since *The Constant Nymph* and have enabled the publisher to print on the wrapper of the second some fair and false recommendations signed by very conspicuous names in English letters. The answer is simply that they contain absolutely nothing that is relevant to our age. They are blankly not contemporary. They might quite well have been written in 1899. This automatically wins them favour, for two reasons. One of them is not so pleasant to contemplate. There is now, due to the very slowly emergent consequences of the war, a very clean-cut division between young and old minds. The books which are liked by people under forty are, as a general rule, not the same as the books which are liked by people over forty; and this means that some of the older writers find themselves diminishing in importance far more rapidly than men who have arrived at such eminence have done during their lifetimes in any other age. They frequently try to arrest the landslide by tampering with our critical standards. They overpraise work done in the old manner (which is naturally followed by second-rate and timid minds) and underpraise work done in the new manner (which is naturally followed by first-rate and audacious minds). By "old manner" I mean the style of the last decade or so, unshorn of the mannerisms which those who have come after have detected; by "new manner" I mean the style the present decade evolves in its attempt to achieve greater precision and harmony than those mannerisms permitted their elders. In any age the new manner passes a harsh judgment on the old, but in this age the judgment is exceptionally harsh, and the reaction of the judged is proportionately more vehement and resentful.

But the second reason is simply this English habit of wandering into the past as a refuge from the distressful present. There is a reason why this should be an English and not a generally European habit. The past we can escape to through our associations is not merely the past, it is peace. Between the Crimean and the South African wars nothing military vexed us save distant consequences of our militarist expansion; and at home we had a succession of steady governments. The same period in France was split across by the War of 1870: and from then until the Great War it had an average of a government a year. Why should the Frenchman exchange unrest for unrest by going back a couple of decades? If he is the kind of neurotic who cannot do with the present he must flee back into a past so remote that it is hard to check claims as to its perfection, and join Benda, Maritain, or Maurras. But the average French critic stays where he is and takes what comes; while the average English critic stays where he was and takes what used to come when he was a boy.

FEMINIST REVOLT,
OLD AND NEW

I HAVE as near neighbours, here in Kensington, three old ladies whose state is typical of the conditions against which the pre-war women rebelled. They can be found at home any morning, three maiden ladies of seventy, seventy-one, seventy-two summers, one practising the harp, one copying on the pastel pages of an album a steel engraving of greyhounds, the third writing in an exercise book a translation of *I Promessi Sposi* in a fine Italian hand. They are so glad to see one, which is no compliment, for they would be glad to see anyone. They know nobody. They have never known anybody. Yet they have obviously plenty of money, they have been beautiful, they are not fools, they have pretty manners. The mystery is explained by the multitude of pictures representing dear Papa, bullet-headed, bearded, bull-eyed Papa, which hang all over the house, and by the adoring anecdotes they tell of

Papa's tyranny and obstinacy. Evidently Papa was one of those monsters of perverse paternal passion not uncommon in the Victorian age who could not endure to share with anyone else not only the affections but even the perceptions of their children. He could claim to be a comrade in arms of the father who acted as Elizabeth Barrett Browning's jailer till she was in her fortieth year. The old-fashioned feminist revolt was against such papas. It demanded liberty for women to gratify their desire for love and work.

I perceive intimations of a newer form of feminist revolt in Mr. Louis Marlowe's *Two Made Their Bed*, a novel which is exciting our English hatred for the contemporary. Reviewer after reviewer has affected not to know where the author can have met people as extraordinary as his characters: yet in fact they are completely typical of the generation that has grown up in Europe since the war, which wants to unpick civilization and make the garment anew, and is undeterred by respect for tradition, since the effect of tradition which is the most obvious to it is the present state of social and economic chaos. The heroine makes a feminist revolt which is completely different from the feminist revolt of the past. She goes further than rebelling against the frustration of the desire for love and work; she rebels against the undisputed sway of the desire for love and work, lest these imperil that essence of the soul which depends on independence. "Can I devise a way by which I can love a man without falling under his domination to the least degree in things either material or spiritual?" she asks. "What is the best way for me to earn my living without surrendering my freedom to my employer or aiding society in its tyrannies over other individuals?" Inspired by this scrupulousness she examines every situation wholly without reference to tradition, as if she were the first woman, and these the first entanglements of man in circumstance.

Any examination of fundamental motives is all to the good, though I must confess that the enterprise strikes me as conducted priggishly, with a doctrinaire rejection not only of the nonintellectual wisdom of the flesh, but of the technique of intellectual wisdom. The heroine has a baby, announces sententiously that she feels no different after from before, expresses dark suspicions that society is trying to put something over on women by falsely alleging that they all have the maternal instinct, and gives her child away to a woman who adopts it. But surely this is to apply to babies the method of approach that lowbrows practise, to their eternal shame and loss, regarding caviare, the music of Bach, and the poetry of John Donne, which resemble babies in that they are repellent to the untutored perceptions of many people but have such a complete accord with the deeper nature of the

human organism that they become the great passion
of those who cultivate a closer acquaintance with
them. Since the human race has had far more op-
portunities of becoming closely acquainted with
babies than with caviare, Bach, or Donne, it has
collected far more testimony to this ultimate effect
on their part than it could possibly collect regarding
the others. It seems odd that a person who would
think it naïve to overlook the limited body of
testimony that urges the giving of prolonged attention to caviare, Bach, and Donne, should think it
the height of sophistication to overlook the far
greater body that makes similar exhortations regarding babies. I do not share Mr. Marlowe's rapt
admiration for the inelastic mind of his heroine and
her fellows, but I can safely affirm that they exist,
that he has drawn them faithfully, and that they are
enormously important. If an American reads *Two
Made Their Bed* he will perhaps understand how it
happens that in an age when there is no enthusiasm
for reformist movements and altruism with all its
works is regarded cynically, the young middle-class
intellectuals will join the proletarians, with whom
they have no interest in common, and vote Labour.
It is not that they have any faith in Marxian or any
other kind of Socialism, so much as that they believe
a Labour government would scrap tradition and
make a fresh start.

THE other Sunday afternoon I fell into the icy darkness of the Savoy Theatre and remained there for four hours, witnessing one of the most star-crossed dress rehearsals I have ever seen, because I could not bear to leave before the end of the play called *Journey's End*, by a new writer, Mr. R. C. Sherriff. I went there because of the urgent representations of John van Druten, who had seen the play at its trial performance by the Stage Society, and who swore that never had he heard dialogue so successfully written in the manner in which the young lions desire to write it. There he was a little wrong. For what Mr. Sherriff does is to write dialogue as all lions, young or old, desire to write it. There is hardly a line which is not strictly relevant to the situation which provokes it and which is not absolutely realistic; and there is hardly a line which does not illuminate the character of the person who

45

speaks it. The dress rehearsal was, as I have said, incredibly calamitous. There were vast deserts of time when scenes were stopped while a tutelary deity named Jim was invoked because there was no mug on the table when the play could not go on unless there was a mug on the table, or while another tutelary deity named George, whose lair was in the ceiling, was begged to make a dawn when dawn should be, but would not. They are, I think, the same tutelary deities that have the circumstances of my own life in charge. But no matter how severely Jim and George continued to prefer chaos, or how playfully chill caught hold of one's toes, the play was indestructible. Its authority maintained itself through all interruptions like the span of a bridge seen through mist.

The subject is the life of five officers in a dugout during forty-eight hours in the fourth year of the war; and it is simply that. In the first act there is a rag of a plot, and not a very good one. It happens that a company officer, a boy of twenty-one, has a young subaltern sent out fresh from home to his platoon; and this subaltern turns out to be a boy of eighteen who was his devoted worshipper at school and is the brother of his fiancée. As the company officer has taken to drink to keep himself going after three years of the agony in the trenches, this is to him a disaster. His alcoholized brain becomes obsessed with a fear that the boy will write home to his sister and tell the truth, and it seems likely for a time that the play may turn into a new version of the Uriah the Hittite tragedy, until the author mercifully decides that it was the cat which brought in this plot and it is the cat which may carry it out. Thereafter, exercising selection but not introducing one shred of extraneous matter, he simply tells what happened in an officers' dugout during the preparation for a big attack. The routine is described, and nothing but the language of routine is used; and the pearls of the Indies could make the effect no richer. There is one scene where a middle-aged officer sits with the boy of eighteen while they are waiting to go over the top on a hopeless raid, and the older man talks to the boy to distract his mind. . . . Alas, poor Zoe Akins! Alas, all dramatists who believe in the picturesque and excitant subject! Strew your stage with palpitant Ethel Barrymores, and flood your backcloth with a terrible light from the sunset of prodigious fornications, and still you shall not wake in our hearts one tithe of the emotion that we felt as we listened to these men in drab suits talking clipped and trite sentences to each other in a hole in the earth.

Yet I cannot say that the play is entirely satisfactory as a work of art. It is enormously impressive and stirring, and in the matters of dialogue and selection it is beyond praise. But I find that, in my own case and in the case of others who saw it at this dress rehearsal, it excites rather than purifies; and I fancy this is because its inspiration is neurotic. Decidedly it is lit by Plutonic fires rather than by the daylight of Apollo. To begin with, it is one more expression of the desperate infantilism characteristic of the modern young Englishman. I do not mean by that to quarrel with his emphasis on the tragedy of murdered youth which was the war's foulest offence, for that is legitimate and most beautifully contrived, particularly at one moment. One had seen the four men sitting in their hell of lice and rats and filth and cold and fatigue and responsibility and fear of sudden death, and sombrely rejoicing because there is one coming to lighten their burden by sharing it. He comes. Slowly he descends the steps into the dugout, he straightens himself, and the light from the candles on the table strikes on his face. Behold! It is a child from school. The man sitting next me half groaned, half whispered, "Eleven days!" When one asked what he meant, during the interval, one was reminded that that actually was the duration of a second lieutenant's life in the trenches: eleven days. That *Journey's End* contains memorable indictments of the world's guilt in this respect one does not complain; but one is disquieted by Mr. Sherriff's assumption that immaturity is the most important phase of existence. The older men in the play are represented as being not only protective to the boys, but deferential to them, as to people of obviously greater importance; and their references to the lives they have left in England are so perfunctory that one realizes the author himself is incapable of believing they could include experiences as exciting and profound as the relationship between the boy of twenty-one and the boy of eighteen, which started at school.

The significance of this can be seen when one considers that there have been three first-rate plays written by young Englishmen since the war— *Prisoners of War*, by J. R. Ackerley; *Young Woodley*, by John van Druten, and this *Journey's End;* and they all have this obsession with immaturity. *Prisoners of War* dealt with a group of young men confined in a neutral country and the prolongation of adolescent affections among them owing to the unnatural conditions; *Young Woodley* dealt tragically with the love of a schoolboy for his schoolmaster's wife; *Journey's End* represents a school friendship as dominating the scene in its reality when all the world dissolves into death and calamity. How very odd this is may be judged if one transposes these subjects into terms of the female sex. If women dramatists were to write plays solemnly setting forth the frenetic sentimentalities of some isolated group of women who got "raves" on each other as schoolgirls do on prefects; the love of a schoolgirl for her headmistress's husband, to whom she wrote sonnets; or a number of young women facing sudden and dreadful death—say in the maternity wards of a hospital—who repeatedly referred to the hockey matches at their old schools and showed that they regarded these as the most important events of their lives—how amazed and amused we should be. This clinging to youth is, however, not merely a division of sex, for I find it puzzles and repels older men as much as it does women. Nor is it a peculiarity of the artistic temperament. In all classes in England one finds men who because they are under forty seem to be bending tenderly over their own cradles. Not long ago I went into the office of a business man and commented on the very beautiful silver box lying on his table, which bore an inscription saying that it had been given to him on his twenty-first birthday. He said coyly, "I shouldn't have it about to show what a baby I am!" The inscription showed that his twenty-first birthday had taken place seven years ago. Surprise made me look like a goldfish.

Infantilism is not a happy state. The childhood of the individual and the race is full of fears, and panic-stricken attempts to avert what is feared by placating the gods with painful sacrifices. For this reason *Journey's End* is a sad play, sadder even than a war play ought to be. There is a moment when the drink-crazed boy of twenty-one is bullying and torturing the boy of eighteen which makes one feel distastefully that one has strayed into a morbid universe, that the author is enjoying the situation, that the atmosphere is tinged with masochism. The drink-crazed boy is not really to blame, for it is responsibility that has turned him to drink. So one can conceive an infatuated child making excuses for a brutal parent in order that he may rationalize his own disposition to submit to his brutality, which is in fact a desire to avail himself of the one and only approach to him. One feels the same despair at Mr. Sherriff's preoccupation with these infantile miseries as when one saw Mr. Ackerley writing across his cartoon of adolescence, "Yes, these are nursery squabbles, but I prefer them to adult life!" or Mr. van Druten's unconscious pleasure because young Woodley had it proved to him that beyond the frontiers of childhood there is nothing as delicate as childhood, and was discouraged. The infantilism of young England is no joke; and it is no affectation that can be slipped off at a moment's notice. For its cause one need not look very far. The process displayed itself more candidly a year or two ago in the still younger generation that were children during the war: as, for example, the little boy who year after year refused to learn to read, and under investigation confided that he did not want to read because reading is a grown-up activity, and he did not want to grow up because grown-up men have to be soldiers. Marvellous how war toughens the fibre of a nation!

IT IS astonishing how the human animal survives
its misfortunes. Evidence to that effect is shown by
the Exhibition of Dutch Art at Burlington House,
which is as glorious a collection of pictures as ever
were housed under one roof before. Reflect that the
Duke of Alba dragged the Spanish harrow of cruelty
through the Netherlands during the second half of
the sixteenth century; that the sieges of Leyden
and Alkmaar were round about 1573; that the independence of Holland was not effective until 1609;
and that all these dates mark stations in such a progress of famine and blood and rapine as this world
has hardly seen surpassed. Then realize that not
a hundred years later the whole immortal crowd
of them—Rembrandt, Jan Steen, Frans Hals, De
Hooch, Cuyp, Ter Borch, and the rest—were painting away as joyously as if they had never heard of
men being other than good fellows, of stomachs
being empty, or of death arriving before ninety.

Historically, the exhibition is astounding. Artistically, it is just such a feast as one's first visit to the Prado in Madrid. The same exultation that experience gives one at finding enough Velasquez, enough El Greco, enough Goya, for one to get a thorough comprehension of their ways of thinking and feeling, was given one here by enough Rembrandts and enough Vermeers. Especially the Vermeers. There are here ten out of the forty-one pictures which are all that he is known to have painted, ten minute and modest renderings of simple things, incomputably precious. They have the same incredible concentration of colour and light in a small compass that one has noted in pools on the road in sunshine after rain. These tactile values are not more dazzling than their moral analysis of the visual experience which is his subject, of refusal to admit any extraneous matter to make its effect more exciting.

After spending as long as I could—for the huge rooms are chockablock with people, since the English have, oddly enough, the greatest regard for the art in which they are least proficient—before The View of Delft, I went home and took down from my shelf Marcel Proust's *La Prisonnière* and read again the description of Bergotte's death. (Bergotte, you remember, was Anatole France.)

Because of a slight attack of uræmia his doctors had told him to rest. But a critic having said that in The

View of Delft by Vermeer (lent by the Museum of The Hague for a Dutch Exhibition) a picture that he adored and thought he knew quite well, there was a tiny bit of yellow wall (which he did not remember) which was so exquisitely painted that it was, if one looked at it by itself, of a self-sufficing beauty like a Chinese work of art, Bergotte ate some potatoes, went out, and visited the Exhibition. As soon as he got to the first steps that he had to climb, he was seized with giddiness. He passed in front of several pictures and had an impression of the staleness and futility of such fictitious art, which could make nothing equal to the breezes and sun of a Venetian palace or a simple house by the sea. At last he came to the Vermeer which he remembered more brilliant, more different from everything he knew, but in which, thanks to the critic's article, he remarked for the first time that there were certain little people in blue, that the gravel was pink, and moreover that there was indeed this tiny bit of yellow wall. His giddiness increased: he fixed his eye, like a child who sees a yellow butterfly that it wants to catch, on the bit of yellow wall. "That is how I ought to have written," he said. "My last books are too dry. I ought to have had on several coats of colour, to have made my sentence a beautiful thing in itself, like that bit of yellow wall." Meanwhile, he was not blind to the seriousness of his attack of giddiness. There appeared before him a heavenly balance. His own life weighed down one of the scales; the other contained the bit of yellow that had been so well painted. He felt he had rashly exchanged the first for the second. "I wouldn't like," he said to himself, "to be among the miscellaneous news of this Exhibition in the evening papers."

He repeated to himself: "A little bit of yellow wall with

a shed, a little bit of yellow wall!" Meanwhile he had sunk onto a circular divan; quite suddenly he stopped thinking that life was a game, and, hurrying back to optimism, said to himself, "This is simply indigestion that I've got from underdone potatoes, it isn't anything." A new attack overcame him, he rolled off the divan to the ground, and all the visitors and the custodians hurried up to him. He was dead.

This passage is packed with information. It conveys the essential qualities of Anatole France: a capacity for perfection greater than his loyalty to it, and an overintellectualized disposition to twist his subjects into amusing and arresting patterns rather than to tell the truth about them. It conveys the essential qualities of Vermeer: a capacity for perfection that walked in step with his loyalty to it, and his reverence for reality. It invents an apt "myth" to represent the dynamic effect of these psychic dispositions. It is a masterpiece of impressionist criticism. Let those who frown on such reflect that Proust had meditated for a diligent lifetime on both Anatole France and Vermeer, and wrote this very shortly before his death, inserting it at the cost of some trouble in an earlier work as if to say that this was a judgment which seemed to him of importance. It is quite possible for impressionist critics to be what they are for the same reason that the impressionist painters were what they were. Having gained complete mastery over their material, they can dare to handle it fearlessly in the ways that will most precisely convey their meaning. To those who have not attained that complete mastery this will seem unjustifiable audacity, and they will make accusations of impudence which are in fact confessions of inefficiency.

THERE· came to London the other day Maurice Ravel, to conduct a concert of his own works. It was not altogether a success, for reasons connected with his temperament. There is something very self-resistant about all his music. It is as if he said: "Yes, there is an infinite deal of music sounding in my ears, but I do not greatly believe in its importance. I will not encourage it by recording it, for I prefer that so far as possible there should be silence"; and as if certain strains insisted on being written down by force of their reality. The soundness of this claim had to be admitted by his exquisite taste, but even so he pruned what he could. When he stood up before his orchestra, a tiny silver-haired man looking like a very small Cairn terrier, it was obvious that this same attitude made him one of the world's worst conductors. He would not hold his orchestra together. He would not help his singer by the marking of a bar line. If the music was to make its point, it had to do so by itself. One witnessed the singular spectacle of one of the most distinguished of European composers showing the most invincible hostility towards sound, even though it was dictated by himself.

Then . . . one went to a party given for M. Ravel by the amiable Gordon Bryan, the pianist. There three people simultaneously played Brahms' Spanish Dances and Wagner's *Valkyrie* music on two pianos while twenty people blew whistles and banged tambourines and beat drums and hit triangles; and ever and anon the host shouted, "Make more noise! A lot more noise!" Why? Because that is what M. Ravel loves to hear, after he has given a concert.

THE English dislike of the contemporary is sometimes thoroughly tiresome. Toller's *Hoppla! Wir Leben!*
has just been produced by our worthy little experimental theatre, The Gate, and was greatly disliked
by the critics, who said it was dull and considered
its theme remote. Yet actually it depicts in German
terms a state of affairs which is one of the most
interesting unresolved phases of English life. He
writes of a German Socialist, sentenced to death for
participation in the post-war revolution and re-
prieved, coming out of the lunatic asylum where
he has been for eight years, ever since the shock of
reprieve unsettled his reason. On his release he
finds the Republic in full working order, and, as
inevitably would happen, is not only disappointed
with the results but also regards every compromise
his comrades have made to get the machine going
as a shameless betrayal of principle. The situation is

in fact extremely relevant to what has happened in
the British Labour party, which has come to a
position of great power just at the point when the
ablest men of the party have become extremely
sceptical as to the practicability of Marxism, with
the result that the slower-witted members (who are
often those who have made the most sacrifices for
the cause) perpetually suspect them of treachery.
It was surely the duty of the critics to give the public
a hint of this appositeness. But they did not. So Mr.
Somerset Maugham's *The Sacred Flame*, which New
York rejected in a fortnight, is cramming its theatre
with audiences directed thither by critics who joy-
fully recognized a play that might have been written at the same time as *The Second Mrs. Tanqueray*,
and *Hoppla! Wir Leben!* had such a short run that
Toller was lucky to find it still holding its own when
he came over to have a look at the London production. If he had been too late, we would have felt
unhappy and ashamed, for his visit was extraordinarily stimulating.

The circumstances of my meeting with him
proved a theory I have long held that to authors of
more than a certain power events present themselves
according to their own style. They begin by in-
venting certain incidents and describing them in
certain ways; and then life says, "Oh, that is how he
likes things to happen, is it? Well, then, they shall

happen to him like that!" An old gentleman told me
many years ago that when he was very young he was
walking in a country lane and met George Meredith
and his first wife on horseback. He expressed surprise to meet them and asked if they lived near
there. Mrs. Meredith pointed her riding switch at a
cottage on a near-by hill, and said, "Yes, that is
our home, the one that has the sun shining on it
now." He tried his young hand at a compliment, and
said, "I am sure the sun is always shining on your
home." The wife and the husband exchanged a long
ironical look, she burst out laughing, her horse took
fright and bolted for a few yards. She reined him up
and walked him away, not looking back at her
husband. A few weeks after she made her elopement
that ended in misery and madness. That is curiously
like an incident in a Meredith novel, and it has
always been my pet exemplar of the theory until I
met Ernst Toller in what might have been a scene
from one of his own plays.

We had arranged to meet at a P. E. N. Club
dinner, but I was unable to get there, so I asked him
to call about eleven at the Ritz, where I was saying
good-bye to some New York friends who were sailing next day. I was in their bedroom when there was
a knock on the door. I opened it and saw a man who
was obviously German. "Are you Herr Toller?" I
asked. He answered, half sincerely, half ironically,

"No, I have not that honour! I am Wertheimer. But they told me Toller would be here." My friends asked him in and sat him down with a drink, and then there was another knock on the door. This time it was Toller, a thin, eager young man with wavy black hair, bearing some resemblance to Charlie Chaplin. I said, "There is a friend of yours here, Herr Wertheimer. He showed no enthusiasm when I took him for you." The two men looked across the room, which was crowded with the towering wardrobe trunks so characteristic of American plutocracy, which gleamed with the silver of the dressing-table set and the silks that were laid on the bed ready for packing. Half sincerely, half ironically he said, "Well, I too would not like Wertheimer to be taken for Toller!" Then they smiled radiantly and shook hands. By that they bridged a gulf. Toller had been President of the Bavarian Communist Republic at the time of the Revolution, and Wertheimer had been one of his ministers. When they were defeated Toller was irreconcilable and was sent to prison for five years; and Wertheimer had taken his liberty and had gone out into the world to work for moderate Socialism. And they had not met since, till this evening in the Ritz. They stood there equals in disillusionment. The only people in the room who still retained faith in revolutionary ideas were my American friends; and so far as one could

see the economic dispensation of this world condemned them inexorably to perpetual possession of
their wardrobe trunks and their silver and their
silk.

It was like a scene from a Toller play afterwards,
too, when we went downstairs to the ballroom and
had supper under the blue sky ceiling of that insipid
apartment, while the pretty women in lace gowns
danced with men handsome as prize cattle. Toller
told us how incensed the governor of his prison
was when he had one day read in the papers that
his prisoner had just published a volume of poems
and realized that the manuscript must have been
smuggled out of prison; and how the old man had
then given a striking demonstration of the peculiari-
ties of the militarist temperament. Most of the
poems dealt with the swallows that built their nests
in the prison windows. So the governor initiated a
campaign against . . . the swallows. Every nest in
the fortress was destroyed by the bayonet. The poor
little swallows built them again and again, but the
governor would not be intimidated. Up raked the
bayonets again and again. One was impressed at
first by the contrast between the surroundings and
the story Toller was telling; and then it occurred to
one that this contrast was not nearly so great as
might have been supposed. The surroundings
turned all they could to favour and to prettiness;

but that he too was doing. Though prisons are solid, a representation of prison life floated past one as lightly as a mist, and though it was gray it was gray only as a mist. Here was another example of a vast gulf between an artist's work and his external experience. Since he was born in Germany just in time to have his youth and early maturity consumed by the war and the establishment of the Republic, life has supplied him with grim and solid blocks of material for his art. But some inner imperative makes him insist on being a lightweight artist. In his plays the ideas of the stage flow over the stage with the graceful precision, the power of forming exquisite momentary patterns, and the same refusal to slow down to the pace associated with the serious which one expects from chorus girls in a good show. It is odd to see wisdom handled with the methods one has so often seen applied to the Follies. Nor am I complaining of it. Delightful it is to encounter anybody who can treat contemporary ideas without embarrassment. There, I think, we have grounds for respecting the Germany of to-day. Toller has obviously a sensitive talent of the sort that might easily be discouraged, but he was obviously helped by his friendly relationship to his own times. One felt that he was part of a culture which knew what was going on all over itself and was therefore as lively as an athlete that has trained himself to coördinate his movements. It would not constantly and sourly disconcert its children (as English culture is apt to do) by pretending that it did not know what they were talking about if they alluded to any ideas younger than the last thirty years.

THE dinner was being given by Mr. Theodore Byard (of Heinemann's) and Mr. Russell Doubleday in honour of Mr. and Mrs. Du Bose Heyward, whose *Porgy* is the admiration of London. Charming as they were (and Mrs. Heyward was looking very beautiful indeed, like a picture by Alfred Stevens, the Belgian, with her dark curling hair which restrains itself from curling too much, lest that should spoil the shape of her head, and her pallor which is like an exquisite physical form of reserve), they were displaced in my mind by the more poignant figure of Mr. Max Beerbohm. He presented himself at the party, looking extraordinarily like one of those little Chinese dragons which are made in the porcelain known as *blanc de Chine*. Like them he has a rounded forehead and eyes that press forward in their eagerness; and his small hands and feet have the neat compactness of paws. His white hair, which sweeps back in trim convolutions like one of these little dragon's manes, his blue eyes, and his skin, which is as clear as a child's, have the gloss of newly washed china. He is, moreover, obviously precious, and not of this world, though relevant to its admiration: a museum piece, if ever there was one.

This evening it could be seen at once that he was not at ease, that he wished himself back again in his rightful home in the Ceramics Department of the South Kensington Museum. He was looking round with surprise, with distaste—and I perceived that his eye was lighting on members of my own sex, on members of my own profession. Yes! He confessed it, in his gentle courteous voice, which has about it something of a Chinese calm, he did not like literary ladies. He did not mind saying as much to me, since I was of course an exceptional woman. One could see the little dragon reflecting that since I was a literary lady I might possibly believe him when he said that. Yes, he repeated, having ventured the bland proviso, he did not like literary ladies. And he had thought he had seen two. Or even three.

At that moment the party really began to arrive. Miss G. B. Stern and Miss Sheila Kaye-Smith came together, followed by Lady Russell (the author of *Elizabeth and Her German Garden*), whose fragile and innocent aspect falsely promises the world that

butter will not melt in her mouth. Then came that
dark Renaissance beauty, Viola Garvin. Then came
Mrs. Belloc Lowndes, the writer of detective stories,
who looks (if you can get the idea) like a pretty
Queen Victoria. Then came Mrs. C. N. William-
son, who seemed to be holding romance firmly to
its place in modern life by a large Juliet cap of
diamonds; and that superb Roman matron, the
author of *Serena Blandish*. They were, I noticed
nervously, coming larger now. The sculptural
splendours of Miss Clemence Dane, darkly draped,
gave the doorway for an instant the air of being a
really handsome memorial to somebody who had
died in a noble cause.

I perceived that on this tide Mr. Beerbohm was
beginning to bob like a cork. It seemed a pity that
he had come. He had no doubt been encouraged to
form other dreams of the evening's personnel by the
invitation cards which had bidden us dine in the
Charles II suite of the Carlton Hotel. I had thought
myself that, in view of the notorious fact that King
Charles's dinner companions were far other than
women writers, this was not too suitable for a literary dinner. When we rose to go to the table, still
more of the dangerous breed pressed in on us. The
average woman writer, I was suddenly conscious,
runs to height and force and mass. More and more
did Mr. Beerbohm seem minute, perilously fragile,
enormously precious. Finally we sat down in our

appointed places, which was at the very end of the immensely long table. But though we were now out of the crowd Mr. Beerbohm was not relieved. Up the long vista travelled the clear blue eye, and remained protruded in horror; for no one, save the All-seeing Eye of Providence, can ever have seen so many women writers at once.

Were we literary women, I inquired of him, like the violets that had been strewn on the tablecloth with prodigality but no very successful decorative effect?—rived from our right place in secluded dells to pursue an æsthetic aim that we never could quite realize? In the faintest of moans he assented. So hypnotic an effect is exerted by the delicate, fixed perfection of his personality, and so single-minded is he in his concentration on the thing which seems to him most beautiful—and that is the society which died with the 'nineties—that I had by now entirely passed over to his state of mind. I found myself lachrymosely remembering the appearance of my father and mother, as I had seen them from my nursery window some time about the beginning of the century, when they walked down the path to a hansom cab that waited to take them to a garden party. Magnificent the hansom cab with its jingling bells; magnificent its driver with his black top hat, his carnation buttonhole, and his beribboned whip. Magnificent my father, as he waved his silver-gray top hat towards the horse. But most magnificent of all was my mother, in her complete dedication to beauty and uselessness.

On a waved plethora of hair, I remember, a large hat rode like a boat, with a bird's wing for its sail; an immense snake of feathers floated round her neck, which was encased in white net supported by invisible whalebones; on her pouched silken bodice she wore a huge bunch of Parma violets upside down; her minute waist was clipped in by a petersham belt; her sleeves were vast bells and her skirts were a vaster bell under which flounces and flounces of stiff silk rattled like silver shrapnel. Her whole appearance, seen in opposition to the soldierly bearing of my father and his relatively simple clothing, cried out, "See how completely ornamental I am. How utterly divorced I am from the idea of the useful! Look, I prove myself by shackling and embellishing myself with this arsenal of garments!" Entrancing world that has departed, entrancing woman! Tears came into my eyes. I could almost smell the hawthorn that had bloomed in our garden that long distant day. I was very willing to admit that, for one accustomed to such hobbled elegancies as my mother's, we women writers must look an uninviting company. Our nearest equivalent in charm was, perhaps, a group of factory chimneys in a northern dawn; or an assembly of Fords at a parking place.

It was just at this point that I suddenly caught sight of Lady——, the wife of a sporting baronet. I felt as if my life—for so strongly had my sympathetic nature identified myself with Mr. Beerbohm's suffering that my life was practically his—were saved. For she is beautiful, but not a beauty of to-day. She does not belong to a past as remote as that which Mr. Beerbohm insists on making his present, but the morning of her flowering was in King Edward VII's reign. Her silver hair springs and curls and coils, unrestrained by that sense of sleek loyalty to the scalp which makes us, her juniors, look so all alike. I am sure that somewhere about her slender form she has concealed a waist which will be brought out in perfect order, should the fashion change. She has that air which only women who were young before the war can achieve, of not understanding machinery and of being able to get on quite well without the knowledge. This enables one to feel that the universe can be, and indeed ought to be, conducted with all the works hidden out of sight round the corner, being looked after by someone else. It indicates a fantasy that the universe need have no works at all, but can just beautifully be projected, the image of a few nice people's minds.

Obviously she was exactly what I—that is, what Mr. Beerbohm wanted. "Look," I said, "there's Lady——." "Oh, where?" asked Mr. Beerbohm. "She is so charming—oh, there!" He sighed. There were perhaps twenty female poets and novelists between them. But at length the dinner came to an end. Mr. Beerbohm stood up hopefully, and Lady —— saw his hope and presently bore down on him with outstretched hand. Alas, the errors we commit, the images of ourselves we smash on the altars in other people's souls, through not knowing precisely what kinds of deities they have chosen to make of us! She approached him with a confidence that came of her belief that at last she had bridged a certain gulf between them, and cried out in her deliciously fresh and jubilant voice, "Mr. Beerbohm, do you know that since I last saw you I have written and published a book?"

Of course the spirit of the age always wins. But since it had won, I thought Mr. Beerbohm might as well make the best of it, so I introduced him to G. B. Stern. With glowing eyes she sat down beside the author whom she admires perhaps more than any other of the living. His courtesy was perfect, his response to her adoration exquisitely gracious; yet the sense that he was not happy in this atmosphere made itself apparent. Impossible for his sensitive interlocutor not to feel guilt at being part of the atmosphere, at belonging so bleakly to to-day. Casting about for a subject to talk about she looked down the immensely long table at Mr. Russell Doubleday, whose extreme slenderness, seen from

MAX BEERBOHM

73

that distance, appeared almost as a vertical straight line. It reminded her of the exercise in perspective one is set in the art class, when one draws lines that stretch away to the vanishing point. Thus it was she came to turn to the most famous living caricaturist and asked him in accents so clear that there could be no possible mistake about what she said, "Did you ever learn to draw, Mr. Beerbohm?" The next day at a lunch party, Mr. John van Druten heard a still, small voice complaining that gooseberries were not so good as they had been when he was a young man; bigger they might be nowadays, but they had not the delicate flavour . . . I need not tell you, ladies and gentlemen, to whom that voice belonged.

In Georges d'Agay's book *Les Aventures d'un Jeune Homme Bien Elevé*, the hero goes for a short space to live in Hell, which he finds indistinguishable from a tenement in Montmartre. On the same storey lives an elderly female demon whom he encounters when she comes in a striped gray flannel dressing gown to draw water from the tap on the landing. Remembering that the saint kept his sainthood, the hero does not quite know what to say; and the demon, reading his silence, says shortly, "There is a dignity attached to history as well as to success, you know, monsieur." Such a dignity, I feel, attaches (in the matter at least of Mr. Max Beerbohm) to myself, Lady——, Miss G. B. Stern, Miss Sheila Kaye-Smith, Mrs. Belloc Lowndes, and the rest of the women writers who so inappropriately gathered in the Charles II suite to meet Mr. and Mrs. Du Bose Heyward.

Most works of art, like most wines, ought to be consumed in the district of their fabrication. In the *New Republic* I read reviews of Siegfried Sassoon's *Memoirs of a Fox-hunting Man* by Mr. T. S. Mathews and of *Journey's End* by Mr. Stark Young, which show how even the most intelligent critics can miss the significance of a work of art through insufficient knowledge of the civilization which produces it. The *Memoirs of a Fox-hunting Man* seemed to Mr. Mathews a straightforward picture of country life which was simple to the point of baldness. Yet in England it was considered to be the most important book of the season next to Virginia Woolf's *Orlando*, and the best critical opinion ranked it far above Mr. Lytton Strachey's *Elizabeth and Essex*. For to us it seemed the most heartrending portrait of a class that was allowed to play at being children until the war came, and then was delivered, bound hand and

75

foot, to the forces of hell. We had been told that there was an almost magical value attached to it. Just as the prosperity of some families is supposed to depend on their preservation in wholeness of something highly frangible, such as a crystal goblet, so the safety of England was supposed to depend on the continued existence of this class. The experience of this view and its supersession in the mind of the writer and the reader gives in itself a twist to the theme, which will be invisible to the reader who is ignorant of this view or has a purely intellectual apprehension of it.

Journey's End, we see, has also left something of itself in England, when we read Mr. Stark Young's opinion that "the picture of dugout life that you get in *Journey's End* has at best the sentimental value of certain sorts of fiction; it is obvious on the face of it that if all the group of men we see there were no more intelligent than they are, there would be more brutality in judging their mental states of mind and more stupidity and cruel lack of imagination; their shadows and lights would be blacker and whiter and their savours stronger." Yet to us English the real theme of the play was the presentation of just such a psychological state as Mr. Stark Young pronounces impossible. We knew that the public schools and grammar schools had worked hard for centuries to produce a class which is not intelligent and not stupid and not brutal; which has no black shadows and no white lights and no strong savours.

Considering these two works together, one recognizes that they have the same theme; the precipitation of a class bred from its beginnings to eschew profundity, into an experience which only the profoundest thinking could render tolerable, with no words to express their agony but the insipid vocabulary of their education, no gods to guide them save the unhelpful gods of Puritan athleticism. They are, however, on a different plane. Siegfried Sassoon's book is a true work of art. It is an analysis of experience and a synthesis of the findings into a unity that excites the reader. Both halves of the process are performed with equal power. He has a wide enough knowledge of the universe to give him a fair clue to the value of the experience. His command over his medium—that is his knowledge of the dynamic effect of words on the imagination—makes him able to convey his opinion about the experience to the reader. Mr. Sherriff, however, properly performs only one half of the process. His subject seems to be the only experience he knows. He seems to have no other body of knowledge concerning the universe which he can use as a basis for comparison. In consequence he does not analyze the experience, he merely reproduces it. His command of his medium certainly enables him to excite his audience by this reproduction, but for all that (it seems to me now that I have seen the play four times) the effect is not wholly satisfying. It is obviously not quite life; it has been subjected to some degree of treatment. It has not been subjected to sufficient treatment for it to take its place in art. Straddling between the worlds of life and art, it cannot find equilibrium.

I BEG all American visitors to England to visit the
Victoria and Albert Museum in South Kensington,
if only to see the one room on the ground floor that
has been lined with the façades and portals of old
buildings: of timbered Tudor houses from old London, of snug little shops that once offered Cornhill
the best soups and jellies, of Palladian mansions
built in that wave of ostentatious expenditure on
country houses which was checked by the American
Revolution. There is one house that I can never
quite believe is really there. It is the front of the
school that John Keats attended at Enfield. Is this
not a little bit like being presented with a posy of
asphodels fresh plucked from the Elysian fields?
For a historic building left *in situ*, unless it can oppose
the modern world mass for mass, as Chartres and
Edinburgh Castle can, is always having its history
scraped off by its impacts with the existence of to-

day. The living will not let the dead lean out from the windows; they push them aside and look down in their much less lovely actuality. We cannot hear the three knocks on the door that announced a visitation of eternal significance because it is forever swung back and forth by those who pass on temporal errands. This schoolhouse is so small that it might easily have been worsted by the present. But here, preserved in this street which is not a street, this room which is not a room, it is magically sealed within the moment of its true importance.

Among the most singular of the fantasies that have from time to time been improvised on international themes, I have always counted chop suey, that dish which introduces a Chinese element to the American gastronomic landscape but is itself unknown in China, and the Femina-Vie Heureuse prizes for imaginative literature. Some time during the war the two Parisian papers, *Femina* and *La Vie Heureuse*, which belong to the same publishing house, decided to give the Entente Cordiale a little something to go on with in the form of an annual prize for the imaginative work of English origin which was best fitted to give France a sympathetic understanding of England if it were translated, and Lord Northcliffe made a reciprocal gesture towards French literature. The choice of the books was to rest with two committees of women writers, one in London and one in Paris. The London committee chooses the three best English books of the year and sends them over to the Paris committee, who selects the prize winner out of the three; and the Paris committee imitates a like routine. What introduces the element of fantasy into the proceedings is that no machinery exists to ensure the translation of the selected work; and, in fact, it hardly ever is translated.

But, in any case, the writer gets fifty pounds, and I for one am always glad that I am a member of the committee, for it brought home to me as nothing else did the appalling effect of the war on the artistic life of the nations involved. For in the early days of the committee there was very little for us to consider. I can remember a certain year when we had much ado to scrape up three books that were worth all this fiddle-faddle of selection and transport. After that famine had been relieved there was for long an un- natural predominance of women writers on our lists, not because our prejudices led us to select them, but simply because the young men had been either killed or temporarily exhausted by the war. One can measure the severity of that interruption to the normal flow of literature now it has resumed. The other day I spent a wet week-end rereading Mr. Evelyn Waugh's *Decline and Fall*, which seems to me one of the few really funny books of our century, and reading for the first time that dazzling exhibition of scholarship and enthusiasm, Mr. Robert Byron's *The Byzantine Achievement*. Both Mr. Waugh and Mr.

Byron are under twenty-six. It is sobering to reflect that had they committed the indiscretion of being born ten years earlier, they would probably be lying dead in the mud somewhere in France, and these books would not be.

To-day the English committee held its annual prize-giving ceremony, which takes place in the Institut Français, a semicollegiate institution where distinguished French authors and politicians give lectures. I myself have sought it but once for these purposes, on which occasion the lecturer (one of the most famous novelists of her country) was prevented from coming at the last moment by an attack of influenza. Yet I did not count the time wasted, for I liked the telegram she sent. For since the French for influenza is *la grippe*, and since she enjoyed only that imperfect command over foreign tongues which is too common among writers, she wrote, "Cannot come, am being gripped in bed." In any case, it is always delightful to visit the Institut, for it is housed in one of those big old-fashioned houses in Kensington which make one understand why, in face of all things, one persists in living in London. Its vast windows look on Thurloe Square, which show such a turbulence of white and purple lilac as I do not believe can be seen so near the heart of any other great city, and its rooms are tall and stately in the Thackerayan manner.

They are good rooms in which to hold a prize

giving, for their proportions somehow presuppose
the regnancy of justice. It was, as a matter of fact,
as just an award as might be. The Northcliffe Prize
(which is now being given by Mr. Jonathan Cape)
was being presented to Madame Lhotte for *Sur les
Fortifs du Paradis*, a novel of French slum life with a
candid attitude towards fundamentals which, were
it practised by any of us English writers, would in-
fallibly lead to a painful interview between our
publishers and a police magistrate. This illustrates
one of the permanent humours of English life, of
which the supreme example was the occasion when
the British Academy entertained one Anatole France
at the very moment that the libraries were organiz-
ing (without protest from the said Academy) a
censorship of fiction on sterner than Bostonian lines.
Madame Lhotte did not appear herself to receive
her prize, but sent as deputy an extremely handsome young man. Those who have attended many
literary gatherings will know that he did not come
amiss.

The Femina-Vie Heureuse prize was being
presented to Mr. H. M. Tomlinson for *Gallions
Reach*. Public celebrations, particularly when they
centre round himself, do not please Mr. Tomlinson.
He is apt, at such times, to resemble a sick monkey
with a beautiful soul, who never bites the keepers
but is fading, fading, fading out of life. But even so
he radiates the charm which he possesses to a greater

extent than almost any other literary man except perhaps Walter de la Mare, and which is a great credit to him, since few literary men have had a more embittering career. When he first emerged as a writer on the sea his emergence happened to coincide with the rise of Joseph Conrad to popular favour; and the fact that they both wrote about these marine matters caused him to be labelled an imitator of Conrad. This was absurd on the face of it. Conrad is (pardonably enough) a loose and inexact writer of English and gets his strength from the images he pulls somehow through the tangle of his language and the rhythm in which he arranges them. Mr. Tomlinson's gift is for the precise use of words which scoop up as much of reality as he desires and leave it on his page. It is, as it were, the art of Turner as against the art of Manet. Such differences in form indicate a difference in essential character.

What that difference was can be deduced from Mr. Tomlinson's pleasure in the quiet, almost imperceptible rhythm of daily life. He is himself not a neurotic; he gives one the impression that he has found the proper sublimation for every impulse he has ever had. He has not that degree of creative genius which makes him interested in lives that are totally unlike his own. He, therefore, does not get swept into those vortices which rage round the attempts of a person or a group of persons to resolve some quarrel with the universe. Conrad, on the other hand, was the centre of such a vortex himself. He was a tortured soul, and his flights from Poland to the sea, from the sea to England, from the life of action to the life of thought, were phases of a conflict that was never resolved. Now, the easiest art form (though not, of course, the exclusively suitable one) for the artist who wants to write about the rhythm of daily life is the essay; and the easiest art form (though one repeats the reservation in this case also) for the artist who wants to write about the vortices of life is the novel. In fact, Mr. Tomlinson is a born essayist, and Conrad was a born novelist. This distinction worked not to Mr. Tomlinson's worldly advantage. The public will not read essays. Therefore he long languished unread, and when he came into his own had to do it through *Gallions Reach*, a fine book, but spoiled by insertion of the conflicts appropriate to a novel by a hand heavy with working against the grain in this matter. Everybody who reads it must give themselves great pleasure; but I wish they would give themselves still greater by turning back to an essay on "Earthshine" in his *Old Junk*, which is unrivalled in its expression of a beauty so subtle that one would have certified it as inexpressible.

What is written in books, I believe from consideration of cases like Mr. Tomlinson's, is not the half of what humanity would write in books if the conditions of this earth were not so cruel-hard a handicap on it. The trouble is that the handicap is a plant that seems to grow in any sort of soil, even when that looks as if it were prepared to nurture nothing but the means to success. The lot of Mr. Tomlinson, who is a member of one of the old seafaring families of East London, but was too physically frail to follow the craft of his fathers, and had therefore to waste his early years as a police-court reporter, and when he broke free found his wit wedded to a literary form not loved by the public—why, that is a lot which obviously a kindly committee of gods on Olympus could alter and blue-pencil to something that could give a better chance to his gifts. But the lot of Sir Anthony Hope Hawkins, who was there to present the prizes, must twenty or thirty years ago have appeared simply not susceptible of improvement. He had every social and educational advantage. He had an early and tremendous success. The vogue of *The Prisoner of Zenda* and *The Dolly Dialogues* transcends anything our generation has known in the extent to which these books dominated the public mind of their time. Moreover, he had magnificent talent. These early Puritanian books are, as a matter of fact, products of an exuberant imagination that at times touches the elder Dumas. Then came the modern novels—*The Great Miss Driver, Second String, Double Harness, The Intrusions of Peggy,* remarkable not only for delicate suavity of technique, but also for the picture they give of the English governing classes. I shall never forget the horror I felt when I first went to the United States and found that the mawkishnesses of Mr. Archibald Marshall were accepted as a true picture of the more prosperous inhabitants of my country. England is not, nor ever was, populated by bread poultices. The Forsytes are better, though they tell not the whole story. But Anthony Hope's novels really tell the truth about the governing class that ran England till the war and has, in its time, thrown up such prodigies as Pitt and Palmerston: insolent, clever, fearless, unscrupulous along certain lines but scrupulous to the death along others, conventional in adherence to certain outward forms and duties but wildly eccentric so far as their own souls were concerned. You have read in *The Education of Henry Adams* how profoundly this class shocked that restrained New Englander when his diplomatic duties took him to London: here is the explanation. Yet although Anthony Hope had this interesting information at his finger ends, and although he had style and taste far beyond his generation, he did not become a great writer, and not one of his books is great. There is no approach to the impressiveness, the authority over the imagination, of *The Forsyte Saga*, though so far as endowment is concerned I will swear that Mr. Galsworthy is not up to Anthony Hope's shoulder. Plainly there exists some handicap.

Of what that might be I got an inkling the other day at this prize giving, when Sir Anthony Hope Hawkins took the chair. To my amazement he was the most completely chairmanish chairman I had ever seen. He, whose command over language is without rival, expressed himself in the clichés that might have been used by the lord lieutenant of any county in England when opening a flower show. Moreover he looked like a lord lieutenant and behaved like one. Like, mark you, the very best sort of lord lieutenant; but I found myself not too pleased that a distinguished artist should look like a lord lieutenant at all. I suddenly found myself thinking of Velasquez. Everybody who has been to the Prado Museum will know the enormous impression which is made at first by the commanding genius of Velasquez; and then the surprise with which one presently finds oneself feeling in front of his pictures an emotion not easily distinguishable from tedium coupled with a disposition to transfer one's regard to the pictures of El Greco. It seems possible that this disparity between Velasquez's endowment and the effect of his work is explained by those passages in his biography which proudly state that so different was he from the general run of artists, so controlled and dignified and aristocratic, that he was treated as a courtier of high rank, and was, indeed, on at least one occasion, entrusted with diplomatic duties. The truer account of the process might be that the aristocracy which he used for his material ended by using him as its material instead. He was so impressed by its qualities that he accepted its standards. Its standards, however, were those of government. They were devised to enable man to deal with the phenomena of the universe in such a way that society will persist. They deal with the organization of the already known. But the artist's standards must be totally different. They must be framed to enable him to analyze the phenomena of the universe, so that more can be known. After a certain stage in his career Velasquez paints like a good governor, using the tried method, exalting the familiar ideal of beauty. Because he is an artist this makes us despondent; for if he, the practitioner of the sole technique for discovery, starts telling the same story over and over again, then we shall never push any further out of the slough where we are. We turn to El Greco, who is pushing on, extending human experience, and relieving us from the fear that man can come to a dead end.

The case of Velasquez is, I fancy, not unanalogous to that of Anthony Hope. He wrote of the English aristocracy without the artist's proper care for his detachment. His books, therefore, became merely the records of its own self-consciousness rather than new discoveries regarding it.

I CAN remember at another prize giving of the Femina-Vie Heureuse gaining a curious sidelight on another writer who seemed to have compromised his relationship with literature by his taste for the pomps and ceremonies of this earth: Sir Edmund Gosse. It was his task two or three years ago to present the prize to poor Mary Webb, and he performed it as mischievously as he sometimes did his public duties. He was the only adult I know of who took advantage of being grown-up as children in the nursery often plan to do. When he felt like kicking and screaming and pulling the cloth off the table, he profited from the fact that there was no longer a Nanny at hand to smack him to put up some naughtiness that was as gratifying.

On this august occasion he let loose those impulses by making a speech in which he expressed his deep-rooted loathing of the whole idea of giving prizes for books, and recorded his melancholy conviction that committees always give such prizes to the authors that least deserve them. It was my duty to propose a vote of thanks to him for this embarrassing effort, and I rose to do it feeling certain that nothing I could say would come very effectively, for obviously he was out to enjoy the occasion. Moreover, a tribute from the likes of me was obviously not the ideal fare for one who notoriously represented the brazenly official side of letters and was maliciously said to revel in his post as Librarian of the House of Lords as much for the sake of the lords involved as of the books.

So without hope of giving pleasure to the object of my homage, and simply because it was true, I recorded the fact that my generation owed a tremendous debt to Sir Edmund Gosse for his exquisite book, *Father and Son*. In that description of his relationship with his father, Philip Gosse, the Fundamentalist naturalist, he set down fearlessly and solemnly the mixture of love and hate which is between parents and children. I did not complete my speech by saying that I felt it extremely odd that anybody who could produce such a masterpiece should come to regard literature as a minor branch of the Civil Service which, when prudently cultivated, blossoms into invitations to Royal Garden Parties. But I admit the thought passed through my mind. I was, therefore, puzzled when he came up to me as soon as the proceedings were over and asked if I had really meant what I had said, and if *Father and Son* had really meant much to my generation. I had, when he came up, been talking to another writer of my own age. We turned to each other in surprise and stammered that of course it had. Both of us were terrified of the naughty and majestic aged child. We thought he was laughing at us. But he amazingly said, "I had no idea . . ."

It was, of course, one of those curious cases where authors of great authority do not realize their power. The star example in this class is Thomas Hardy, who knew he was a great poet but could never quite believe that he had convinced the world of it, and always submitted his work to editors in quite honest expectation that he might quite possibly be rebuffed. But I stumbled on an even more interesting aspect of Gosse's artistic situation by adding that I was a great admirer of his one essay at fiction *The Secret of Narcisse* and had read it over and over again when I was a schoolgirl. That seemed to astonish him, and he asked eagerly if I had read it in more recent years. Yes, I had. So too had the other writer. And did we still think it was good? Of course we did. Timidly, for we were both frightened to death of him, we added that it seemed head and shoulders above what was being written at that time. He expressed pleasure at our judgment so generously that I should have suspected he was laughing at us if his old age had not shown indubitable signs of emotion.

I could not understand this incident until a year or two later when, in making some researches for a lecture, I turned up some literary papers of the early 'nineties and found the clue. Young Gosse had made a reputation as a critic during the 'eighties. He had then produced his first attempt at a novel. The cheap and obvious thing which the small mind longs to say of a critic's creative work is that, though he can pick holes in other people's work, he himself lacks the vital spark which enables them to do that work, such as it is. The small minds of 1892 said that cheap and obvious thing over and over again about the charming and graceful *Secret of Narcisse*. Gosse, having been made the most diffident of creatures by the home he described in *Father and Son*, believed them. He was betrayed into doing so by the circumstance that as he was an inflexibly honest man who had never written a malicious review in his life he imagined that all other critics were as high minded. So absolutely did he accept the verdict of his ineptitude as a novelist that he never attempted fiction again. It is probable, therefore, that his naughty irritability proceeded from the damming of a creative impulse which was strong enough to have needed full play; and his concern for titles and rank was not plain snobbery, but a pathetic attempt to associate himself with the eminence of others because the eminence which was appropriate to himself had been judged out of his reach. I have never known a more startling example of how potently vile spite is once it is admitted into criticism; nor a more convincing proof that a characteristic which seems unlovable when considered by itself, can be the consequence of a drama which, fully comprehended, compels sympathy and liking.

"And where," said I, "shall we lunch?" For we had motored out to fetch a friend whose work forced him to spend the summer in a dead and alive town in the greenest vacuity of rural England, seventy miles or so north of London; and the answer to the question was by no means obvious. "Let us go to Boddington," said my friend. "Don't you remember? It's the place we went through three weeks ago on the way to the Oxford Road, with the figures of a king and queen on the church tower." "The fact that a place has a church tower with the figures of a king and queen on it is no guarantee it will provide a decent lunch," objected the Third. "Quite so, but if it does not provide a decent lunch," said the Second, "we can console ourselves by looking at the figures of a king and queen on the church tower. For let us not forget that there are ever so many

96

places which will give us a bad lunch (this being
England) and which have no church tower with the
figures of a king and queen on it for us to look at
afterwards." "Bless you, my lad," said the Third—
for the Second is still in his teens—"you have begun
to learn how to live."

Thus, steering by the twin lights of hope and
despair, we started to make our way cross country
to the Oxford Road. More than once we stopped to
inquire for Boddington, at a village store under
thatched eaves that sold pink-drill corsets and pep-
permint balls in jars marked "Curiously Strong,"
and from dairymaids on whose cheeks the glow of
health was so vivid and concentrated that in a
London night club it would have passed for the
most perverse and insolent make-up. And, oh, my
astonishing country! Nowhere could we find a soul
who had heard of Boddington. Yet, when we found
it, much later in the day, it proved to be not fifteen
miles distant. But let no one leap to the conclusion
that this proves the vacancy of the rural mind. Far
from it. The truth is that in England the rural mind
is weighed down by a superfluity of geographical
names. Every field and every spinney has its proper
and by now arbitrary name. The field which the
stranger will know as the one with the three ash trees
standing on the knoll is known to the village as
Parker's Field, and its neighbour with the bramble
thicket round the pond is Barron's Field; and who

Parker and Barron were not a soul out of the church-
yard can tell.

It is possible, therefore, that the minds of the
storekeeper and the dairymaids were as crowded
with as great a quantity of geographical detail,
albeit it referred to a confined area, as the rest of
us had collected during fairly extensive travels in
Europe and America. Vacuity the trouble was not;
and its practical consequences did not worry us in
the least, since in front of the village store was a
round pond by which three laburnum trees let
down their golden hair, and the dairymaids loitered
on the threshold of an avenue of pink and white
chestnut trees. I cannot deny that to reside in my
native land is for the most part like living under a
shower. But there is usually about a week in May
when England beats the world for beflowered and
verdant prettiness; and this was it. Moreover, we
lunched long before we got to Boddington. Greed
overcame us.

Yes, it was sheer greed, for we had breakfasted
late. It is disconcerting for those of us who desire a
universe obedient to neat Kantian principle to see
how often gratification of our baser emotions brings
on us the most exquisite and even ennobling experiences, and vice versa. Years ago, I remember,
a lady doing settlement work in the East End of
London told me how difficult she found it to deal

with the Jews because they had such queer ideas;
and she cited with lowered voice a factory girl who,
after she had attended a course in English history,
announced that the most striking lesson she had
learned from her studies was that Charles I never
would have had his head cut off if he had restricted
himself to the same pursuits as Charles II. I feel
as disconcerted by my own reflection that no virtuous and self-sacrificing action of my life has ever
brought me as immediate a delight as that I owe
to the weak and gluttonous desire to get hold of some
cold meat as soon as possible which drove me into
the (let us say) Smithers Arms: that dull though
trim little inn at the end of the village about which
there was nothing at all distinguished except the
uniform apricot tree that was trained up the front
of every house.

My delight, as those will readily guess who have
eaten at wayside inns in England, had nothing to
do with the lunch. That, as I had anticipated, consisted of cold mutton that was very sheerly sheep, a
cucumber and some tomatoes stark in a glass dish,
gooseberry tart, a crusty loaf, and sweet butter.
"The kind of lunch that Wordsworth would have
liked," said the Third severely to the Second, who
was grumbling. "Yes, but that's why one doesn't
like Wordsworth," responded the Second. The good
time began after lunch, when the landlord, a quiet

man, came in and told us that he had permission to take his guests over the grounds of—yes, I shall go on using the name Smithers, for plainly I must not direct anybody to this spot; and indeed it was just such a simple, downright English name—Smithers Hall. Without excitement, for while not wishing to boast we can fairly say that we have been about a bit, we accepted his offer. He picked up his cloth cap from an oak chest in the hall. We stepped out into the sunlight on the dusty road. A pink-eyed mongrel, whose appearance made a confused assertion that there was a pack of foxhounds in the neighbourhood, slunk at our heels. "Ah, get along with you!" said the landlord. "I don't want you with me now." Not till he bent and feigned to throw a stone would the highly irregular tail wag away in the right direction.

A gateway opened into a circular drive that ran round a very ordinary shrubbery. From the road nothing could be seen but the shrubbery. When one had entered one saw that the drive led to a solid, sensible, not very large Jacobean house, to which there had been added on each side a wing done in the Adam style by someone much less gifted than the Adams. In the middle of each of these wings, set in the wall a little above the ground, was a large black stone bearing an inscription. Idly, for we were still not very much interested, we strolled up to look at them. In florid, peruqued lettering the inscription

began: *Ludovici Jussu* . . . Ludovicus? Ludovicus
who? "A Mr. Smithers brought these 'ome with
'im," said the landlord. "Not *this* Mr. Smithers. Ah,
get along with you!" The pink-eyed mongrel had
made a reappearance and had to be threatened into
flight again. By this time we had read the inscription; also an explanatory line that had been painted
above it at a later date. "Oh, I like Mr. Smithers,"
said the Second. For Ludovicus was no mean
Ludovicus: he came of a line of as important Ludovici as the world has ever seen, that had specialized
in Jussus. He was Louis XV, and these were the
foundation stones he had laid in the pier he built at
Cherbourg. For it had happened that in 1758 Mr.
Smithers, being an admiral of the British fleet, was
sent to take Cherbourg and destroy the pier, and had
not been unmindful of his back garden in Northamp-
tonshire when he did so. Next time your liner waits
outside Cherbourg and you see the breakers dashing
over the mole, think how home-loving Mr. Smithers
waited there in his time, and how he reacted to
Ludovici Jussu. "The Smithers family 'ave bin about
a lot, they 'ave," said the landlord, and led us
round the house to the terrace.

The house stood on the side of a broad and shal-
low valley, the existence of which could not be
guessed from the highroad. The whole valley, which
must have been three miles across, was a park.
The grass was like a lawn, and herds of deer browsed

in the shade of exquisitely disposed groves. "It seems a pity," said the landlord, with what none of us took as irrelevance, "that there's only one Mr. Smithers left: the young one that's at Oxford. All his four brothers were killed in the war." We turned towards the house and looked straight into a library that is as it was when it was first furnished and the wing new built. By the window peonies in a Kien Lung vase spiralled with dragons dropped red petals on a walnut bureau. Its proportions were so perfect that one could hardly believe the original maker responsible for them, since he must have been a mortal liable to err like the rest of us and felt that time itself must have applied the last shaping. The shadows of the room were finely fluted with innumerable old books, and the nearer light fell on the beautiful pale shades which seas and continents assume when they have floated on the globes in gentlemen's libraries for a century or two.

"There was a Mr. Smithers who was quite a scholar," said the landlord. "I've 'eard tell there was .an author called Gibbon used to come and stay with the family. Would you pass along and look at the 'all? Mr. Smithers wouldn't mind. Anybody I bring is all right." We looked through the window at an Italian bahut of ebony and ivory inlay that drew a strange beast on every drawer; an early oak chest like one there is at Knole; a chair or two of the kind that Chippendale made and sent to China

to be lacquered; and on the wall at the back one of
those cups of sweet-chocolate-and-whipped-cream
that Murillo chose to call by the name of Assump-
tions of the Blessed Virgin. "A Mr. Smithers," said
the landlord, "was an ambassador in Madrid once,
long ago. Oh, go 'way, you!" For the pink-eyed
mongrel was with us again.

We walked through rose gardens, and a man of
seventy-five smiled at us with clear eyes. "His
people," said the landlord, "have always worked
for Mr. Smithers." We went through woods where
bluebells lay as if the spring floods had been of
flowers this year, to an avenue of stupendously
stout and gnarled yew trees. The yew is the sacred
British tree, and an ancient growth of them is as
likely as not to mark a place that had significance
for the imagination of past peoples. This was a
niche on the hills that may have given an impress
over desolation when the country was undrained
and fenny. We came out on a summerhouse that
some cheerful, sporting Mr. Smithers had built of
mud and decorated with patterns made of thousands
and thousands of fox bones, set high on a mound by
the park boundary, so that one could see far over
the agricultural demesne, neat as a new pin, that
stretched westward. "Eight miles the property runs
this way and seven miles the other," said the landlord. "Ah, you pesky little varmint!" But he spoke
lovingly to the pink-eyed mongrel, for really there

was no sense in trying to pretend that this was a
world which was not very kind to little dogs, being
far too sleek in its well-being to insist peevishly on
the conditions of breed that it theoretically exacts.

After that we went along an avenue of beeches,
each one a king among trees, and passed a vicarage
which, we were told, was occupied by Mr. Smithers's uncle. "The living belongs to the family, and it
always goes to a younger son, so the vicar's always
been a Mr. Smithers, just as the squire's always
been a Mr. Smithers." The church was disconcerting; for with the exception of its tower, which
was debased Perpendicular, it exactly resembled
Mr. Smithers's house without variation from that
extremely secular pattern. "You see," explained the
landlord, "the church was burned down about 1770,
so Mr. Smithers had it rebuilt to match his home."
Was it the same Mr. Smithers who had brought the
Ludovici Jussu stones? Yes, it was. Mr. Smithers,
throughout the ages you have always been good,
but in that particular incarnation you were specially superb! Mr. Smithers, I adore you as passionately as is possible considering the intervention of
time, the great chaperon.

Within the church, not so good. Mr. Smithers
had apparently fallen a victim to the Evangelical
movement which swept aristocracy and working
class alike at the end of the eighteenth and the beginning of the nineteenth centuries. Every expres-

sion of the religious instinct that might be described as Papist had been banished, with the result that the church was very like a whitewashed barn. Its sole ornaments were marble tablets on which black letters told laconically (since there are some things that can be taken for granted) the virtues of deceased Mr. Smitherses and their wives. The particulars of these consorts opened vistas into history the world over. One was the daughter of the fifteenth Earl of Spillikins. *Ay de mi!* The Spillikinses have fallen on evil days. The present Earl of Spillikins (the nineteenth) is one of the leaders among the blue-blooded settlers in Kenya Colony, which we took from the Germans during the Great War. He spends his time voicing the claim of his kind that they shall be able to force native labour to work on their plantations; and the Colonial Office, being corrupted by democratic control at home, will do no such manly thing, but performs instead cantrips which turn the stomachs of the gallant gentlemen—as, for instance, sending out anthropologists trained in the Jungian school to investigate native customs and beliefs.

Some there were, too, who belonged to systems that had not been granted even such a discouraging measure of survival. One Mr. Smithers of the mid-eighteenth century married a French duchess, and you know how that world ended. Another, in the early nineteenth century, married an Austrian

baroness; whose kin are as like as not teaching dancing at hotels in Carlsbad. "And Mr. Smithers's
mother," said the landlord, "was an Italian princess
before she came to us"; and he spoke the name of a
famous Italian family, of the sort whose effeteness
has been proved by the triumph of Mussolini. What
delicious scenes must have led up to these international alliances! Consider the quietly dressed
stranger coming to the gates of the gloomy palace
and (after presentation of the unquestionable letters
of introduction) being taken past scores of flunkies
by the major-domo to the audience chamber of the
descendant of all princes that have ever reigned.
"Your Highness, I wish to propose myself for the
hand of your daughter." "And who may you be?"
"I, sir, am Mr. Smithers."

Elsewhere in the church was remembrance of
another kind of travel. On a tomb by the altar, an
evident relic of the old church, lay an alabaster
Crusader. "Is that the tomb of the family that
lived here before the Smithers?" I asked. The landlord looked surprised. "No family lived here before
the Smithers," he said. "Didn't you notice what a
funny name our village has?" I had. "It's the
Anglo-Saxon name, and they say it's never been
changed because the property has always belonged
to the same family. When William the Conqueror
came over there was a . . ." He paused. A faint
smile appeared on his face. I sympathized with his

dilemma. It did seem absurd to use the term about somebody who had died nearly a thousand years ago, but what are you to do? He said it boldly: " . . . there was a Mr. Smithers living just where the new house is to-day. . . ."

Driving home we said, "How curious it is that we are on the eve of a general election! There has not been the least sign of interest in one single town or village we have passed through." A jackass rubbed its long ears against a barn door with no alteration in its manner (which was that of one trying to remember the exact quotation) because there was posted from hinge to latch a poster printed in the True Blue of Conservatism. An ash tree raised its sticky black buds above a hedge, and one was impressed by its resemblance in combined grace and rigidity to the best wrought ironwork, rather than by the poster on the gate beside it, though this announced that a Labour candidate was standing for a constituency where twenty-five years ago a workman suspected of Socialist sympathies would have been turned out of his cottage into the streets. We agreed sagely that people were so indifferent because they all knew exactly what was going to happen. "No change at all," said the cynical Second. "A slightly reduced Conservative majority," said the cautious Third. "A substantially reduced majority," said I, but only for the reason (please do not laugh at me too loudly) that I cherished a belief in the Liberal party's power to stage an impressive come-back. Mr. Lloyd George's unemployment scheme looked not so bad beside his Tory opponents' total lack of ideas. The emptiness of the Grand Canyon moved a humorist to acclaim it as the perfect place for one's used razor blades, but that was only because he had never looked into the mind of the English Conservative party. Mr. Lloyd George's performance also compared well with the Labour party's doings, because it proceeded from conviction, whereas Mr. Macdonald and his friends have in their hearts lost all faith in their own formulas. Setting aside these trifling variations, we all agreed that we had never known a tamer and more prognosticable general election; and we reverted to talk of the ineffable, the pervasive, the eternal Mr. Smithers.

This calm persisted even on Election Day. I voted on my way to the opera, and thought no more about it. In the entr'acte of *Don Giovanni*, when we stood about in the Covent Garden foyer, which is nearly as enchanting an island of the past in the present as the foyer of the Comédie Française, we did not talk of politics. We talked of the extreme satisfaction given by Elisabeth Schumann, who seems to launch the whole of herself at a note like something which is plumper than an arrow but which has the arrow's power of flight; and of the extreme dissatisfaction given by the amazing Covent

Garden tradition of accompanying all the recita-
tives in *Don Giovanni* on the piano. We would all
have gone to our beds without another thought of
votes had it not been for a party that even I, who no
longer stay up of nights, felt ought not to be altogether missed: an election party.

They took us up in the elevator, those poor little
dears in the white boleros and Turkish trousers,
fresh creatures clad in the uniforms of faded fancy.
Some day, I thought, as we flashed past floor after
floor of the immense department store, where
merchandise assumed the outlines of great statuary
under dust sheets, we will have a world-wide revolt
of the usherettes. "Why did you dress us so ro-
mantically," they will say, "when nothing romantic
ever happens?" We stepped out of the elevator to the
chaste halls where for six days out of the week the
not too grand and not too gay sit and eat that eighth
part of a waffle which in this benighted country is
mockingly known as waffles, that tenth part of a
portion of ice cream which is as mockingly known as
an ice, and drink the tea which it is their birthright
to like. It was at once evident that the temperate
genius of the place was ousted. Men in white clothes
with coral necklaces hanging to their waists and
musical instruments in leather cases hung about in
perturbation. They were a Hawaiian band who had
been engaged to play, but they could not find out
where they were to play, and in the search they had

found five other bands performing. Through their complaint passed a slimness in white satin like many another. Her face bore that defiant determination to look like everybody else which marks the inverted rebellion of the rebellious royalty. Beyond, people danced on a floor that gleamed towards infinity. Lady Oxford, that curious totem pole, spun alone among the dancers. It was perhaps the quickest way of getting across the floor.

Through a doorway men in green baize aprons were hammering and sawing away at a huge turntable. Ultimately champion skaters danced on it. Incongruity was so definitely a quality of the evening that I should not have been surprised if it had been me and the Princess Ingrid and one of the lost Hawaiians who had to do that. Through another doorway passed a couple of sporting peers with rose-coloured faces and that lost, glaucous look in the eyes which denotes those who have given their human kingdom for a horse. Were their faces a deeper rose than usual, did a concern for human interests flop about in their eyes like a fish out of water? In the room beyond were tables holding up innumerable champagne bottles to the glory of the Lord and the wonder of man. At the first table sat a woman of squat physique who nevertheless had a dominant air of sitting higher than her audience; and indeed there held her up, wherever she sat, the moneybags of an immense fortune garnered in London and

New York. Her audience was Fania Marinoff, tiny
and shapely and brilliant and exotically coloured,
like one of her own dazzling finger nails, and Carl
van Vechten, who has been greatly beloved in
England ever since he had a long illness in the Carlton Hotel and held levees there, dressed in vermilion
brocade pajamas on a bed covered with a jade
Chinese shawl, gorgeous as a Tiepolo. Over Carl
was bending our white-haired host, Mr. Selfridge,
who has carried his passion for international blend-
ings to the point of becoming almost exactly like
Mr. Lloyd George. In motherly accents he was in-
quiring, "Are you sure you've got enough to drink?"
Behind him the radiance of hundreds of electric
lights reflected on the thousands of champagne
bottles imitated the lighting of the heavens.
(Though, by the way, not a soul was drunk.)

One went back into the ballroom, where Noel
Coward was. "But aren't there election results being
shown somewhere?" "There." He nodded his head
towards a colonnade, behind which were rows and
rows of the flat black fiddle-shaped backs of well-
groomed Englishmen, the flat, floured backs, rising
from printed chiffon, of well-groomed Englishwomen. They were all turned one way, and they
were held tense. As one looked they relaxed, a
tremor ran through the rows, and there burst out a
storm of boos. We had not time to tell each other
that that must have been a Labour victory before

we spun round on our heels. For through the windows behind us came the sound of a cheer from the people in the street below, which rushed up and licked the tall building like a flame. We went to the casements and leaned out into the night. The whole of Oxford Street in front of Selfridge's store, and for some distance on each side of it, with the exception of the narrowest possible alleyway for automobiles, was packed with people whose families had always worked for Mr. Smithers. Their faces were upturned to a vast lighted sheet let down over the façade which showed the state of the polls. Many of them had been there since half-past eight, and it was now after midnight. They were there because they cared. Heavens, how they cared! When they cheered, it sounded as if the cheers came from deep down in their guts and tore their throats.

"The Labour people are in, you know, they're definitely in. Isn't this terribly like the French Revolution with us booing inside and the crowd cheering outside?" The comparison, though often made during the evening, did not strike me as particularly apt. The ballroom was by then dominated by one of the Dolly Sisters. A floating gown of tender green chiffon deserted each shoulder in turn as she demonstrated good will to all she met with forearms encased in emerald and diamond bracelets continuous as drainpipes. Emeralds and diamonds swung from her ears, emeralds and diamonds flung a wide loop about her neck and bosom, as she practised an immense display of vitality divorced from any cultural or even human associations. It was like going over an engineering plant and opening a huge door and finding a dynamo spinning its magics. Near by stood Mr. Michael Arlen, looking in some indefinable way like some Dolly Brother. Almost especially he did not remind me of Versailles.

I went up on the roof and walked for a while among the lovely lawns and flower beds that have been planted there by our really remarkable host. It was a coldish night, and none were there save a few lovers. In the tulip garden only a handsome boy, square-shouldered and tall as they are preferred in the Guards, drooped with a little golden curlicue of a girl over a sundial. From the leisurely and enjoyed melancholy of their attitude one might surmise that they were fearing lest this new dispensation should prevent them from being perfectly and eternally happy, as otherwise they would certainly have been. The yew hedges planted round the parapets were so high that one could not see into the street below, but the cheers rushed up past us into space. They went so fast that they must have caught up with the music of *Don Giovanni* as it slowly mounted from Covent Garden to the stars. But of course they would not go up so far, not the whole way, as the music does. In a lull between the cheers I heard a sound from the northern quarter of the night. People came up to me just then, and I tried to tell them about it, but they wanted me to hurry downstairs to a new phase of the party.

Everybody in London was there now. All the princes and princesses that are far enough from the throne to go to good parties; the beautiful picture-book men and women of the foreign diplomatic corps; all kinds of rich people, all kinds of clever people; the entire casts of most of the successful plays in London, who sat together, so that one felt as if one were moving through several imaginary societies as well as through several real societies. The cast of P. G. Wodehouse's *Baa, Baa, Black Sheep* sat in one corner, and one instinctively laughed as one passed, feeling that here everything would be turned to a grave silliness which is a cool and stoical defiance of the limitations of human life; just as one looked apprehensively at the cast of G. B. Stern's *The Matriarch* as they sat in a fan round the enormous naughtiness of Mrs. Patrick Campbell and expected them to break into Viennese-Jewish paroxysms at the election results. But those were no longer being given. This Conservative assembly, which had just received the totally unexpected news that (as it sees it) its class was threatened with extinction, sat in the utmost good temper while the issue of the election results was suspended, the screen rolled up, and the stage behind given over to a boxing match between a man and a kangaroo.

Yes, they sat and laughed and clapped and cheered, and told each other that the kangaroo really loved it. Though as the kangaroo staggered about the ring, giving back the blows flatly because it had learned from experience that that was what was expected of it, its sad small face delivered a moving election address of its own. "I am that which never has power," it said. "I am that which cannot make money, own banks, nor sit in offices, nor govern armies, nor live in big houses, nor fight for its own hand. If you only wouldn't do this sort of thing to us! I don't want to be pushed into this ring, and have all these bright lights turned on me, and hear you laughing at me. And though it is the essence of me that I am not important, somehow what you do to me is of the highest importance. Don't you see that the same thing that makes you cruel to me makes you cruel to each other? Watch me, watch me, I am the clue to all your secret misery, compared to which the outward woes inflicted by a government are but little things!" His paws flipped forward in their great boxing gloves, his head rolled back and he assumed the incomprehensible and significant expression of a holy martyr.

Surely it was time we left, for it had begun to be light. One could imagine dawn sitting in a drowsy heap beside the driver on one of the market carts that would now be creaking their way along the highroads into London. The crowd outside had gone. A Labour government, as it learned with a tiresome finality the last time Mr. Ramsay Macdonald held office, does nothing at all to one's obligation to show up at the office in the morning on time. The English guests of Mr. Selfridge stood and shook hands and said in the same level tones, "This is the best party I've ever been at. Well, I suppose we're all ruined now." Americans said with more animation, "It certainly has been a wonderful party. But isn't this terribly exciting! Poor old Conservative England!"

I had it in my mind to tell them what I had heard on the roof, but it really was getting very late. But if I had told them my news, and they had known enough of English history to credit it, they would have been enormously relieved. For what I had heard on the roof was the sound, faint but unmistakable, of Mr. Smithers going Labour. How do you think he has managed to keep his very desirable corner of England to himself for so nearly a thousand years, while Stephen chased Matilda round the counties, and the Wars of the Roses broke the mould of daily life, and the Reformation and the Civil War forbade men to sleep in their beds, and the House of Hanover put the Stuarts to sleep? The answer is something like adaptability, only more so. Nothing, nothing in the world, will ever unseat Mr. Smithers from the saddle he means to ride. English perpetualism (which the foreigner is apt to mistake for Conservatism) will not fight Socialism, it will permeate it and mitigate it. Remember those foundation stones that were laid to support Cherbourg pier, that ended in the wall of an English country house.

Attasmithers!

WHEN I left London for Provence some amusing things were happening in London. There were, for example, some art exhibitions that were exciting the town. The first exposed the paintings of a Spaniard called Señor Beltran-Massés to the gaze of a metropolis which might have remained stonily indifferent had not our popular press been shocked by those which represent the female form. I must explain that the purity of England has been immensely affected by the orange. The tone of the *Daily Express* and the *Sunday Express*, those self-constituted guardians of our morality, is set by one Mr. James Douglas, who used to be a cheerful newspaper man until he was overcome by a serious illness and was sent to a famous sanatorium, at which he was allowed no form of nourishment throughout a period of many weeks save orange juice. He returned in perfect health but in a state of extreme moral delicacy.

Sometimes this works out to the detriment of the exciting stimulus; since Miss Radclyffe Hall is sincere and well bred, no financial gain would make the prosecution of *The Well of Loneliness* anything but a veritable martyrdom to her. But at other times it works out very well indeed for the offender.

I myself sought admission to the said exhibition of Señor Beltran-Massés's paintings, but lost heart at the sight of a queue that stretched from the gallery door for a couple of blocks. For some time I stood fascinated by the spectacle. Not only was it that I had had no idea the female form was still worth that much in our city; it was also that I was receiving food for my delight in the interplay of forces between nation and nation, from sea to sea. It is surely very beautiful that Señor Beltran-Massés, child of the land of the orange, should profit from a reaction set up in Mr. James Douglas by the use of the orange.

Señor Beltran-Massés's pictures, I gather from such as did see them and from reproductions, were guileless enough representations of females with circular purple shadows round the eyes and long green-white limbs, resting under midnight skies more thickly strewn with stars than is astronomically probable, after having been drawn backward through some hedge of passion: the kind of painting one is more accustomed to eat under to music than to go and look at cold in a picture gallery. But Señor

Beltran-Massés himself is a pleasing phenomenon. When he was presiding over the first day of his show, shorn as carefully as a poodle (though not of course in the same way) and tailored so gorgeously that the morning stars clapped their hands together, one of the most intelligent journalists in London eyed him and decided that this was a personality worth watching, particularly in view of certain events connected with the opening ceremony. For Mr. James Dougglas's papers might perhaps not so readily have directed their inflamed susceptibilities towards these pictures had not Señor Beltran-Massés adopted a very curious attitude to one of his own canvases. It represented Salome, that poor girl who has received more attention from second-rate artists than any of her sex save the embittered females who sit about the Café du Dom and the Select; and its painter oddly chose to announce with the utmost publicity that it would be removed from the private view of the exhibition, in order to save the Spanish Ambassador (who was opening it) any embarrassment. "This," said the journalist to himself, "is a card, if I mistake not." He approached the painter and said, "I would like to have a word with you, Señor Beltran-Massés, if you can give me five minutes when the reception is over." The painter smiled, gave a charming bow, and said, "Oh, yes, I like your England very much. It is so beautiful a country." "I would like," repeated the journalist, "to have five minutes alone with you, when you leave the show." "Ah, yes," said the painter, bowing and smiling again, "and I admire so much your beautiful, long, slim Englishwomen."

Observe the initial misapprehension which led him to suppose that English people would ask him how he liked England. In point of fact, no Englishman ever asks a foreigner that question. We are an arrogant and a stoical nation. We think that a stranger is bound to like England if he has any sense, and if he hasn't it's no use having his opinion; and if he has found out anything wrong with the place presumably it can't be altered or it would have been long ago, so there's no use talking about it. Moreover, the Englishman is pretty critical of England himself, as men are of women they know themselves bound to by an unbreakable bond of passion; and they feel a like resentment of the outsider who tries to join such criticism. In this misapprehension one sees a failure to grasp reality which will forever prevent him from painting other than badly. In his method of dealing with the situation arising out of this misapprehension one sees a certain quality which accounts for his bravura style. What abundance of that equipment which leads straight to beautiful studios with lots of tiger skins and Persian rugs and antiques and a musicians' gallery and duchesses on tap! There, I feel sure, goes a really happy man. I do not know what the moral of this is.

The journalist told me that story when we stood together in another picture show that has caused a stir in London and excited the sad imbiber of acids. Mr. D. H. Lawrence's exhibition of pictures at Dorothy Warren's gallery in Maddox Street, at the corner of George Street, Hanover Square. And the picture we stood under reminded him of another story, which went to prove that the universe is really a strange place, and Señor Beltran-Massés and his works foam flecks on a dark stream. It was called Fight with an Amazon, and it represented one of Mr. Lawrence's earth-mother women binding up the wrist of one of his fire-virile men while a pack of wolves looked up at them. "Those wolves remind me," said the journalist; and he told me that a friend of his had been describing to him an experiment he had seen demonstrated in Paris by a pupil of Pavlov's. Heaven knows what exactly had happened, for I distrust all nonscientific accounts of the scientific. But in the tale as it was told me a wolf hound had been brought in and chloroformed and then decapitated. Its head was put on a plate, and there it remained for half an hour. Then the large veins of the head were joined by tubing to an artificial heart in a tank. And lo! the head, that had been dead, lived again. Offered food, it accepted it.

Offered acid, it rejected it. Its eyes, its jaws, its tongue, its ears, made just such patterns of communication as they had done all its life. "It looked up, they said," the journalist told me, "like one of those wolves." And when the tubes were cut it died a second time.

"How interesting," said I. "But of course of no real psychological interest till it's done on a human subject, who can speak." "You can be sure," said the journalist, "that those Russians have thought of that. There will be one at least of those men making up his mind to offer himself for the experiment." Yes, of course it would be so. We both were silent as we meditated on the strange and terrible situation in which, without doubt, one of our fellow creatures found himself at the moment. If one believed it to be one's highest destiny to add to humanity's knowledge regarding the physiology of the brain, then one would feel it one's duty to dive down into death, come up again for just that hopeless minute and no longer, and then go back. Completely novel dilemma with which man has vexed himself! And consider, too, that since most of the people likely to make this experiment would be enthusiastic believers in a mechanist philosophy, one might witness the sight of a Lazarus raised from the dead to announce with shining face the mortality of the soul.

Very appropriate it was that we should contem-

plate the strangeness of a universe where we cut off
the heads of dogs and men and will do anything in
the world, even to going down to death, rather than
live peacefully, since we were standing in a gallery
hung with the productions of Mr. Lawrence's most
uneasy genius. The exhibition was both intensely
interesting and disappointing. The pictures were all
of nudes, and though they were all far less ec-
centrically conceived and more dexterously ex-
ecuted than we would have anticipated, they were
also much less pleasing. Mr. Lawrence seems to
have very pink friends. It is true that there is one
quite lovely Leda, and that in the background of a
canvas illustrating the Boccaccio story of the convent gardener there is a bit of composition involving fruit trees in blossom and the nuns' broad
straw hats, which recalls the finest descriptive passages in his prose and verse. But on the whole the
exhibition presented that mixture of strength and
monotony one had thought characteristic of weakness, that combined vehemence and poverty of
imagination, which one has noticed a thousand
times in his writings. It is as if he were tethered to a
few images by the umbilical cord of some infantile
interest which will not let him range the wide
domain that ought to be the subject matter of such
genius; and those images, having to bear the full
force of that genius, become bent out of shape under
the excessive burden.

The trouble is, too, that these images are not straightforward representations of the subjects that really concern him, but disguises his mind puts up because it cannot bear to contemplate the causes of its distress. The ostensible subjects of his pictures are always these virile men, these maternal women, engaged in these semi-murderous assertions of vitality among themselves with which his books have made us familiar. In his preface to a book of reproductions of these paintings he declares that he painted them to represent the human body in the splendour which the modern spirit of shame has taken from it; and he alleges that this shame is a consequence of the introduction of syphilis into Europe at the close of the Middle Ages. Man, according to this theory, looked down on his rotting body and felt spleen and hatred against the cause of his corruption. This is, of course, partly true. But one wonders at its being put forward as of such importance, when the ritual fussiness about sex (such as the ceremony for purification after childbirth) in the Old Testament, to take but one example of the thousands offered by the pre-syphilitic past, proves that shame is a more primitive and less logical emotion than that. Mr. Lawrence's eagerness to make an external episode account for what is evidently an event in the interior life of man makes one suspicious of his attitude. One becomes more so when one finds that the net impression of this exhi-

bition, consciously designed to uphold the pride of
the body and kill shame, is one of collapsing pink-
nesses, of the flesh at its most hopeless and helpless
and abased—in fact, at its most shameful. There is
plainly some terrific distortion going on in Mr.
Lawrence's mind. He will not name the real subject
of his conflicts; and when one looks at these canvases, one feels that he spends himself on these harsh
and monotonous celebrations of vitality to distract
himself from a constant preoccupation with physical
failure and death.

Yet what a man! How much better is it to be willing to have one's head cut off, in the sense of sever-
ing oneself from the easily comprehensible, and to go
down into the darkness of the not yet comprehended,
than to be like Señor Beltran-Massés! Moreover this
show reveals him as one of those supermen, like
Goethe, who can turn their hands to anything. For
mind you, these pictures are real paintings. The
most recent of them, a study of an Italian peasant
stripped to the waist, is technically brilliant. England has a right to be proud of him.

. . . At the precise moment I was writing these
words, my sleek-headed new *femme de chambre* came
into my room in the Mediterranean villa where I
happen to be and announced, having cast down her
eyes and assumed her enchanting air of being about
to recite a poem in rhymed couplets, that lunch was

served. By my plate was the *Continental Daily Mail*, in which I read that six plain-clothes policemen had entered the exhibition of Mr. D. H. Lawrence's pictures and removed thirteen of them from the hooks and had taken them away. Loathsome incident! To begin with, there is an infuriating lack of symmetry about it. Six shocked policemen ought to take twelve pictures; that odd one is an offense. But the stupidity of it! The pointlessness of it! Was it the Leda which provoked the authorities? Surely they must grasp that it is no use trying to keep dark Leda's peculiar ornithological interests. That secret got out years ago, centuries ago. You can no more suppress it now than you can get a gas escape back into the tap. For the rest, the prosecution of these pictures is a grave injustice to men, for the most they did was to depict the male form with some of the flattering particularity which is taken for granted in representations of the female form. None of these pictures could have put a morally improper idea into the head of man or woman. The only harm they could possibly do is to cause embarrassment to children at the sensitive ages when they avert their attention from the physical signs of sex; but nothing is more unlikely than that anybody not fully adult should attend a picture exhibition open during term time within school hours. The thing is an appalling indiscretion considering that Mr.

D. H. Lawrence is perhaps the greatest genius of his times, and is so ridiculously sensitive that this is as likely as not to cause a temporary paralysis of his work.

I T WAS the permanent officialdom of England which was responsible for the recent and extremely unpopular award of the Order of Merit to Mr. John Galsworthy as successor to Thomas Hardy. It should by right have gone either to Mr. George Bernard Shaw or Mr. H. G. Wells. These are writers greatly superior to Mr. Galsworthy in artistic merit, and of infinitely greater importance to their times. The award to George Bernard Shaw would have been enormously popular. I have recently had an insight into the place he holds in the affections of the English public through an unimportant part I play on the board of an English weekly journal called *Time and Tide*. We have only to publish an article by Mr. Shaw, no matter on what subject, for our circulation (which is already healthy) to be immediately doubled. There is no other writer who can do this. In fact, he has performed exactly the

achievement of which the Order of Merit is supposed to be the recognition. He has put forward
certain ideas and modes of thought which have
proved their validity to the satisfaction of the people,
who now employ them with the gratitude of those
who find themselves possessed of new and useful
tools. To him rightfully belongs the honour; and had
he refused the honour it should have gone to Mr.
Wells. He too has performed that achievement. If
one took a census among young and middle-aged
men who have reached positions of eminence in any
department of life, and asked them what author had
had the largest part in inspiring them to their exceptional attainments, an overwhelming majority
would give the name of H. G. Wells.

It may be thought that to be agitated because
neither of these writers received the honour is to
fuss about nothing, to worry because the duchess
does not call. But in a country like England, which
is largely governed by a hierarchy based on the idea
of social service, it is very necessary that now and
then a flat assertion should be made to the soldiers
and sailors and administrators that literature also
can make the supreme claim that it upholds civilization and saves man from extinction. Hence it is
infuriating when the Order of Merit is withheld
from both the persons who preëminently deserved it,
for no other reason than that they were closely
identified with radical movements displeasing to the

permanent officials in whose hands, at the last
resort, is the bestowal of such honours; and when it
is given to a writer of such definitely inferior attainments as Mr. Galsworthy.

There is no homage too extravagant to be paid to
Mr. Galsworthy as a man. His integrity is so flawless
that it seems as absurd to mention it as it would be to
point out that there are no cracks in the firmament.
He is a spring of kindness that never runs dry. If
one were to write a list of his beneficences, in the
way of dutiful attendance on committees and
personal service to unhappy individuals, it would
hardly be believed. Truly, the man is an angel. But
his work is minor. It is not profound, it copies the
world rather than interprets it. The precise function
of *The Forsyte Saga* was historical: it recorded the
moment when the middle classes of England, though
their wealth and power were founded on capitalism,
found themselves forced by their sternly cultivated
honesty to admit that there was a great deal of
justice in the intellectuals' criticisms of the effects
of that system on human happiness as a whole. It
has many counterparts in the innumerable books
which were written in France during the latter
part of the eighteenth century by members of the
ancien régime who had to admit that Rousseau and
the Encyclopædists had convinced them against
their own interests. But once he had finished that
particular job (which, one hastens to acknowledge,

was a burdensome one exquisitely performed) his intellect was not sufficiently powerful nor his insight into the souls of men profound enough for him to find another subject. The latter portions of *The Forsyte Saga*, where he has attempted to depict the younger generation, have already been hopelessly outclassed by Miss. F. Mayor, whose admirable *The Rector's Daughter* and *The Squire's Daughter* I again beg all American readers to obtain. For the rest . . .

For the rest it occurs to me that it is not really permanent officialdom which is to blame for Mr. Galsworthy's election to the Order of Merit; it is the perfectly appalling state of English criticism, which permits the older generation to lay a dead hand on the literature of to-day. The work of any author who had acquired prestige before the war (and of any author who from timidity expresses himself in terms of the last generation) is sacrosanct. The other day Mr. Galsworthy produced an extremely poor play called *Exiled*. The London theatre-going public knew that it was terrible. It is no fool. For proof of that, see how it packs the door of His Majesty's Theatre to see the Guitrys, and how it streams out of St. James's Theatre, laughing and chattering as only very pleased audiences do, after it has seen the dazzling performances of Lynn Fontanne and Alfred Lunt in the Theatre Guild's production of *Caprice*. The ill-mannered among the first night audience of *Exiled* expressed their opinion frankly, and I have met nobody who saw it and did not deplore it. But the soft-pedalling of the press on the subject went far beyond the natural impulse of decent people to be generous to a man who has done better work in his time. It amounted to a declaration that such an author is entitled to have his productions indiscriminately praised forever and ever so long as he lives. This is a beautiful act of loyalty, but what is to happen to the public taste if it is perpetually invited to admire poor work? Particularly when it is invited to regard anything new, even if it is of the first order, like Cocteau's *Orphée*, with sulky contempt. In fact, literature is lying down on its master's grave and refusing all food.

I BROKE my journey south and spent a day in the Ile de France, watching the soft warm rain of June fall on the long waters in front of turreted châteaux. There France seemed the land of temperance, of measured delights, with an infinite power to calm both by its landscape and its language. For how naturally French falls into phrases that have the soothing calm of nursery rhythms, that give comfort simply by the foreordained quality of their rhythms! On the market place of Rambouillet there is a notice *"Lait de la ferme de la folie."* That would be a good thing to say over and over again when one cannot sleep, just as the gray-blue poplar glades formality has set so wisely in the park of Rambouillet would be good to remember in any moment when one had permitted life to fall into disorder.

But when I left the train at Marseilles I knew France to be, on the contrary, the land of harsh and superb excess. I motored over mountains from which there rose, stranger and infinitely more beautiful than any scent the perfumers can make, the incense of pines nearly as hot as if they were burning on a heath, of sunburned rosemary, of a thousand herbs macerated by the hammer thud of day after day of intense heat. All along the rocky beds of dry torrents the full-fleshed rosy flowers of the oleanders gesticulated defiantly at the heavens as if to declare that they have their own secret for sustaining their own magnificence, no matter what the sun may do. Excess is the only way by which this land can fight the violent destiny brought on it by its longitude and latitude, the extremes of which were now manifest before me in the present heat, and in the devastation left by the frosts of the past winter.

That devastation I realized most poignantly when I passed the villa I lived in two years ago. The palm avenue, under which one could stand at noon and know a cool night of shadow, is an assemblage of clothes-props with a few leaves fluttering gawkily at the top. Gray ghosts stood horrid in the sunlight, and they were all that was left of the mimosas that had pressed against my balcony a florist's livelihood of golden flowers. There were yet taller and more terrible ghosts, and these were the eucalyptuses that had in the past seemed to give a solid promise of longevity, since in the south they had attained the solidity which most trees cannot achieve save in the north. Gone is the undergrowth in which my three ginger cats were able to live with the secrecy of tigers in the jungle, a state very gratifying to the feline soul, so that they eyed me insolently when they came to feed, and would permit no liberties. There, in fact, the villa stands naked save for a few haggard pines, as if it had lost its clothes in a fire and had only been able to save a few of the family canes and umbrellas. Yes, the frost has burned the countryside exactly as if it were a fire.

What a time Provence has had of late! Two years ago there was the unprecedented season of forest fires that brought ruin and infinite terror. In a village in the foothills not far from here the people were roused from their beds one night and went quietly, with that civil discipline which is one of the most extraordinary (and most hidden from the casual view) qualities of the French, to take the last sacrament, in case the wind did not drop in time and the circle of fire that enclosed them contracted to its centre. Then last summer there was a burning African drought; and later the frost came to show that cold can be crueller than heat. It is no wonder that when one is driving along the road and meets an old peasant driving his cart, the face one sees under his wide-brimmed hat is usually frenetic, the mouth under the white moustache gaping open as if under perpetual strain, the eyes, pale in contrast to the burnt skin, bulging like a frightened animal's.

Poverty is not the determinant factor in making him what he is. He is an excessive type, bred by this land of excess. The rope-lank and smileless peasants that one sees in the Cévennes, if one takes the road from Nîmes to Paris by Alais and Villefort, are more what poverty does on its own. It is a bad road, that, from the motorist's point of view; but it is one of the most beautiful roads in the world, as it winds among the mountains that are like gardens with their apple orchards and chestnut groves, and hold up to the sun on their high passes stout château-fortresses a thousand years old. How different it and its people are from the trim vineyards of the Rhône and Burgundy, and the plump, technically pre-occupied, but never hurried vintners, which are what one gets on the road to Paris! Yet that, too, is not the undisputed terrain of peace. The war against phylloxera, had it been waged against human enemies, would have been set down in the history books as a gruelling campaign. Every part of France has its difference and its difficulty. Even the Ile de France, for all that its genius is essentially temperate, has intemperance thrust on it by the unsolved political problem of France. It is the miracle among miracles that out of this complexity of dissimilars, each of them forced to be very marked in its dissimilarity in order to cope with the problems peculiar to its environment, should arise the unity of French civilization.

THE villa I have taken belongs to an old opera singer, and in the bookshelves I find bound volumes of *Le Théâtre* going back for the last thirty years or so. When my cook Jasmine came in for one of those intimate talks one has with one's servants in this country, I showed her the photograph of a famous French vaudeville star of the beginning of this century, a creature of dark and efficacious magic, and told her that I had had a childish passion for this woman, that I had slept with her photograph under my pillow, and that I had very seriously begged in my prayers that I might grow up to look like her. "Oh," said Jasmine, "how was it that you didn't know she had the villa opposite you when you were here two years ago? She's old now, and in a terrible state. She's lost nearly all her money gambling, and the rest of it goes to a young lover she's got, and he gives it all to another woman, who's young and pretty. Why, she owes such a lot of money to the tradesmen in the village that they won't send her any more goods. Her cook often used to come round and rap on my kitchen door and beg for a bit of bread, because the baker wouldn't trust them for another crumb, and I used to let her have it. But then she came wanting some butter, and that I couldn't give her. Oh, no, madame, I would never be so careless of your interests as to give her your butter! Bread, now, no one minds giving away a little bread, but butter, you can rest assured I would never give away any of your butter!"

So I suppose it is true that Helen of Troy was a leper in her old age and begged from door to door.

For a sad and sudden reason I found myself obliged to spend an evening in a town of which I knew I had heard, but of which I could remember nothing: Tournus in the department of Saône-et-Loire. As I went into the dining room of the little inn called *Du Sauvage*, I passed a girl in the doorway who peered down through the fading light at the pages of a guide book and said gaily to someone whose face was a smear of pallor by her shoulder: *"Oui, c'est vraiment le lieu de sa naissance . . ."*

I went in and sat down, and as I waited I stared out into the courtyard, which was still light, for the passage out of it looked straight into the sunset. Immediately I perceived that it was not a court-yard, it was a stage, on which a performance then and there began. There was only one performer, but that was enough. She was about ten years old, and some of the fringe on her forehead seemed to have been touched by a brushful of gold paint, and the rest was the light bronze brown of bud cases. Her very light eyes were neither gray nor blue but the colour of summer airs, and her cheeks and chin had the round but imponderable contours of small clouds and the white blandness of standing milk. She had in her hands two roses, which I do not doubt the minx had stolen for these exhibitionist purposes, and throughout the whole time I sat at dinner she brought these into constantly changing relationships with her beauty. Now she set them behind her ear, now she laid them at the base of her short throat, now she held them at her breast so that I could see how she looked with her eyes downcast. She should, I suppose, have been smacked for her vanity, but I am glad she was not, for she was as exquisite as she thought she was, and she placed herself to make a picture within the frame of the window with the most perfect taste. Now, whose birthplace do you suppose I fond Tournus to be, when I went upstairs and consulted my *Guide Bleu?* Jean Baptiste Greuze, none less. I must have struck the contemporary representative of a long line of narcissistic wenches, one of whom had in her day determined the subjects which should always remain in the gifted lad's imagination haloed with the glow belonging to pleasantness early perceived.

THE reason I was delayed at Tournus had to do with the chauffeur of the car I have hired for the summer. He is not now so strong as a bull, though his mother made him so, since he had been sub- jected to the operations of history and gassed at the Marne; and he had gone down like a ninepin with pneumonia under a cold wind that had yawned on us for a minute as we crossed the Hautes Alpes. For the next day and the next he had refused to admit that he was ill, though his sickness was like a layer of gray paint on his sunburnt floridity, and had driven me at an insane speed across France as though he hoped to find a town where he might leave his fever and then another where he could be quite well again. Nothing I could say would stop him, though from the first onset of his illness he had given me that uneasy visceral sensation that comes when one sees anybody full of life, even a comparative stranger, invaded by the shadowy fluid of death. I had to wait until he collapsed; and that he did at Tournus.

That little town happens to possess one of the most splendid Romanesque churches in Europe. Between consultations with the doctor I went out and took a taste of it, following the alley that runs between the two fat towers that were built to ward off the Hun invasion in the tenth century. (Odd it was to remember at the sight of them that the whole of civilization has passed through crises as precarious as that on which the chauffeur's life now hung by a hair.) Heavy rain was falling in Burgundy; the gutters were so full fed that they looked like runnels of gray glass. It would not seem likely that I should need the refreshment of going into a dark, cool place; yet as I went into the church I felt much as I do when I walk over the red dust of my garden under the brassy sky and slip off the rocks into the green Mediterranean to swim among the gold and silver fishes. It gave one relief from some condition present in the outer world. I walked with comfort among the high, blunted arches of the nave and crypt and narthex, that were built close on a thousand years ago, that will be standing a thousand years hence. A side of it was dominated by a Madonna cut out of cedar wood so long ago that it was very close to the Byzantine mode. Her face was painted nearly as dark as the soil of the country, the fluted and gilded folds of her robe covered a body square like a cupboard, and in front of her she held a stiff little Christ like a puppet she had taken out of that cupboard and would doubtless put back at the end of the day. Behind the altar ran an ambulatory, the vaults and chapels that opened off it making vague, lofty, mothering curves, borrowing the forms in which the human body expresses tenderness and rendering them non-decadent in the substance of stone. In the crypt pillars shaped like the strength of man purged of all its grossness held up a chapel roof shaped comfortably and defensively like the womb, but dark and cool, innocent of the disturbances of light and heat and all that they engender. At one end was the altar on which the body of Christ was and is and will be mystically transformed again and again to bread and wine that was somehow the same as living flesh; and at the other end was the tomb of a man who, though not divine, had transcended all human calculation and eternally benefitted by death, since he had been elevated to sainthood by his martyrdom.

Considering these altars, I realized the source of my comfort. I had come out of a world wholly committed to life, which regarded death solely as an enemy to be contended with, into the expression of a world which accepted the idea of death and played with it. Those who built the church no doubt thought of it purely in architectural and theological terms, but there was a dream at their elbows. It is true, said this dream, that man goes from his birth under the shadow of death, but let us build an edifice that shall symbolize this aspect of his fate and show it noble. Its pillars and walls shall meet aloft in arches and vaults so that he shall always have over him a curve like the rounded head of a coffin, and they shall shut out the light of common day, as coffins do; and the whole shall be beautiful, and the repository of all the ideas that through ethics and philosophy try to impose order on the seething phenomena of life. It shall be decorated by images that represent a birth memorable because it led to a death unparalleled in its glory, and shall proliferate into chapels that mimic the enclosing safety of the womb but make no threat of future trouble. Part of it shall be dug out of the earth underfoot, like the grave itself, we shall make tombs as real as any that man shall ever fill. Some of these tombs will be mystically inhabited by our God who knows how to live again, and others by the bones of men who offered themselves up to death and were rewarded by eternal blessedness, by a kind of being more intense and ecstatic than mere life. If there is a part of man which remains sceptical of these unproved assertions, let it be persuaded by the peace that enters into this building when we have driven out of it all activities characteristic of the everyday world. We will interpret the idea of death in every conceivable mystical and rationalist sense, but that will be the whole of our dealings with variety, for to that one idea we will remain entirely faithful.

Death, indeed, was the subject matter of mediæval man's art and thought to an extent that is almost incomprehensible to the modern mind. To-morrow, as soon as I had put my chauffeur under proper care, I would go to Dijon, a curious journey, like travelling through a wine list, for I would pass through or near the villages of Meursault and Montrachet and Pommard and Volnay and Beaune and Nuits-St. Georges and Vougeot and Chambertin. Dijon itself is like a wine cellar, for there, too, time has meant ripening and not decay. As the sweetness made by past weather and this rich soil stands in the vintner's bottles, so the beauty made by history and this rich soil stands in the streets of the fine old town. There is the Cathedral, which soars up in the pure aspiration that the thirteenth-century builders knew, but is covered on its floor with terrible bewigged statues of the seventeenth and eighteenth centuries, pursy with pomp, as if they had mumps. It is as if the stream of life had shot up in a high ethereal spray and then rolled down the walls in round gross drops. There are the mediæval houses that have flagged courtyards complete with galleries and spiral staircases up round towers, robust and right. Not so right, but still good, are the Renaissance houses, ornate as if in those days stone could be embroidered like fine lawn, and they had put many waiting women to the task. There are the graver eighteenth-century houses, one of which is very grave indeed behind its great door and its high wall, because there Buffon bent his wig over a thousand volumes and soberly thought along a way that was to lead to as many revolutionary changes as if the thinking had been as rash as you please. Among a congeries of such houses is Notre Dame, that superb condensation of the mediæval genius, that baffling declaration of the gulf between that age and ours. It was built in the twelfth century, so its interior is even purer than the Cathedral. Stone has never been more chaste, a more appropriate celebration of the Blessed Virgin. But when those who built it came to decorating the exterior they sent for a genius who was that age's equivalent of James Joyce, and said, "You know that idea you had about Leopold Bloom? Just express it all over the façade, please." So three lines of grotesques look forth and say in unforgettable terms what genius knew and felt of man's disposition to wallow, of the sensuality which is the cause and the enemy of his fine thoughts about chastity. Stone has never been more gross. How the intervening centuries have refined us! We would never think of defiling the public mind by building such an exterior to a holy place. It is un-

fortunate that the process of our refinement seems
at the same time to have robbed us of the power to
build such an interior.

Different and more beautiful than our day's doings is what we see in Dijon; and, at its finest, an
expression of this different attitude towards death.
That finest is now segregated in the museum, which
its presence makes as well worth visiting as any in
France. The traveller must forbear to spend too
long pondering over the mystery of the canvases
representing curled and blonde nudes and signed
"Charles Chaplin," but dated in the eighteen
eighties; or on the macromegalous productions of
the local sculptor (whose colossal bronze bust,
cryptically inscribed "F. Rude," is the first object
one sees when entering the town) who during the
first half of the nineteenth century never wearied in
representing the abstract virtues as damn fine
women. He is responsible for the figures in high
relief on the base of the Arc de Triomphe. Passing
by these distractions, the traveller must go to the
room chiefly reserved for the two supreme masterpieces of Burgundian sculpture. They are both
tombs. On one, two angels kneel at the head of
Philip the Bold, holding his helmet till he wakes,
and on the other, four do like offices for John the
Fearless and Margaret of Bavaria. Every circumstance connected with those personages is expressed
to the fullest. In the slender and palpitant gold

wings of the angels is all that the early Gothic age thought of heaven, in the lions at the monarch's feet all that it knew of heraldic pomp; the prostrate figures are as royalty had to be to maintain itself in chaotic Europe. But the artists (for there were several of them) were ambitious to do more than that. Under the slabs on which the monarchs lie are miniature cloisters in which monks stand cowled, weeping for the dead. Is that all they are? Indeed it is not. They are brave monks. Many of them are persisting with the business of life: they pray, they read, they hold up the symbols of their authority. But always their cowls engulf their heads and shoulders, their hoods smother them, their cloaks and robes swathe them, and within these swaddling clothes they are bowed and shaken by their grief. In fact, they represent man doing his best to live, although he is confined and frustrated at every point by the limitations imposed on him by death, and aghast at his knowledge of them. Just as the church at Tournus expresses man's relationship to death by objective symbols, so these figures express it subjectively. It cannot sufficiently be emphasized that death is the sole subject of this masterpiece, and that it is not morbid. It is, on the contrary, more sturdily virile than anything man has sculptured since.

Just a couple of hours or so before I came to Tournus I had paid a visit to the famous church of

Brou, which is, so to speak, the child of these two tombs. Margaret of Austria built it about fifty years after the tomb of John the Fearless and Margaret of Bavaria was finished, to be a casket for the bodies of her husband, Philibert le Beau, her mother-in-law, Margaret of Bourbon, and herself. If it is a little too precious and expert, if there is something in its facility that recalls the energy of high fever, it is nevertheless very beautiful. The building itself is exquisite in colour, being pearly and pale amber, like an onion skin, and the intricacies of the screen are disposed with the perfect felicity of buds on a branch in springtime. And it, too, is entirely dominated by the idea of death. Church though it is, the climax of the building is simply and solely the three tombs in the choir, which occupy so much space and have so much to say for themselves that the most the Persons of the Christian religion can do is to maintain an inconspicuous presence on the retables on the walls. The absorption in the subject is as great as in Tournus or on the tombs at Dijon, but the method of regarding it is different. There it was the relationship of death to man in general that was considered; but here it is the relationship of death to certain human beings in particular that agitates the artist. These tombs are relevant to the mortality of the rich and powerful, and to no one else.

The cherubs who stand languidly beneath Margaret of Bourbon's tomb, supporting emblems of bereavement, are pretty pages, attendants on a court that knew its airs and graces to be more permanent institutions than any grief; the hooded mourners are court ladies who wear their skirts full in order that they may drop wide curtseys to earthly monarchs. The death of an aging dowager does not, however, cut very deep. The tomb erected to a sovereign levelled in his prime expresses a more awe-stricken reaction. Can it be that all this magnificence known as Philibert le Beau has suddenly stopped? It appears that it has; and, now one comes to think of it, all human magnificence is liable to such sudden cessation. Brooding on that, the artist carved that figure which, in a desperate attempt to make a completely secular work of art relevant to what is theoretically the subject matter of all contents of a church, is called "Mary Magdalene before her conversion," but which represents any sensual schoolgirl in the soft might of her young flesh. In the mind's ear one can hear her inflexible voluptuousness passing resolutely and without haste from pleasure to pleasure, like a bumblebee droning from flower to flower. That magnificence can be arrested by death, the artist notes in wonder; and so can the determined and decorous fruitfulness of the mother who shields her rounded body with the homespun folds of her gown at the other corner of the tomb. The catastrophe is so vast that one can

almost enjoy it, the interest it arouses takes away the
terror. Since death in its hostility towards magnificence has not spared our magnificent prince, says
the artist, growing a little maudlin, let us give him a
magnificence that death cannot touch, since it is
carved in incorruptible stone; and so the tomb becomes encrusted by purely compensatory ornament.
In the third tomb, erected to the energetic woman
responsible for the whole building, this maudlin
mood becomes blowsy. The decoration becomes
fuddled in its determination to heap wreaths on the
corpse who has been sequestered from flowers in the
coffin, to clothe in richness the skeleton who has
been stripped of that primary vestment the flesh.
Death is no longer considered either objectively or
subjectively as a whole. All the artist deals with
here is an unimportant and immediate emotional
reaction to a particular instance of dying, which is
in itself a flight from death, an attempt to escape
from its sting by sacrificial rites. The light of art
stands over Dijon at high noon; here it slants from
the sunset.

The situation put before us by these sculptures
is remarkably odd, judged by the standards we
apply to our own age. If a school of divinely gifted
sculptors should arise in the United States it would
be startling if they devoted themselves for the next
hundred years or so to carving tombs for President
Coolidge, Mrs. Coolidge, and Mr. and Mrs. John

Coolidge. No one would blame them if somewhere about the middle of Mrs. Coolidge they began to grow cold. Even to imagine such a preoccupation binding the lifetime of a single artist is incredible. If Mr. Ralph Wright had spent most of his career making a mausoleum at Woodlawn Cemetery we would mock at his morbidity and pertinacity. A mere sequence, did it cover the same ground as "The Dance of Death" on which the mediæval artists were always trying their hands, would set the critics shaking their heads over the mental state of the party responsible. The subject has been shooed out of the sphere of the pictorial arts, and indeed, out of the spheres of all the other arts too. Literature knows nothing of it now. None of us dare say with Prospero, "Every third thought shall be my grave. . . ." If an essayist such as Drummond of Hawthornden should produce a crape-edged little brochure on mortality like "A Cypress Grove," no publisher would jump at it. A preacher-poet in circumstances equivalent to those of John Donne, enjoying (let us say) a pastorate in Park Avenue and a contract with Harper's, would do best not to lament "'Tis lost, to trust a tomb with such a guest," and to rejoice that "The *Lord of Life* was the first that named *Death*." Otherwise he would be urged by his vestry and Mr. Thomas B. Wells alike to recuperatory tours in the Holy Land, to medical treatments aiming at the purification of the internal

economy. Is it not the accusation against Charles
Dickens that his characters indulge overmuch in
the pleasures of pathetic and premature decease
which finishes him with the young? Death as a subject lingered longest in the theatre. I myself in childhood saw Sarah Bernhardt ride her vitality at the
task of conveying its extinction like a weatherbeaten
huntress clearing a gate, not once but half a dozen
times. But those days are gone. I have never seen a
threat against the longevity of Miss Gladys Cooper,
Miss Lynn Fontanne, Miss Eva Le Gallienne, or any
other English and American star of recent years.
The only first-rate play I can think of written in
our time with death for its subject is Jean Cocteau's
Orphée; and though it is probably the best play of
this century, it aroused among the critics the peculiar irritated disapprobation which stupid people
feel for something that stands apart from the spirit of
their age.

What is the cause of this change in man's attitude?
Why do we exclude death from art? We feel no more
reconciled to the idea of dying than ever we did.
When I found out at Tournus the degree of my
chauffeur's illness both our faces were gray. Fear
was tearing at his vitals and mine too, although I
had employed him for so short a time that till now
he had been only a shape at the driving wheel. No,
we have not lost our interested awe at death. Is it
that we are in a position to slap ourselves on the

back and say that we have laid aside our morbidity and now place our creative impulses at the service of life and not death? Assuredly it is not. Just as we seem to have lost the power to build the interior of Notre Dame and evoke the white aspiring angels of earth, at the same time that we forewent the power to build the exterior of Notre Dame and evoke its dark engendering angels, so we seem to have lost a good part of our power to represent life when we ceased to represent death. It is surely not mere coincidence that the decadence of Burgundian sculpture coincided with its failure to face the idea of mortality. The trouble lay, one may suppose, in man's twofold reaction of courage and cowardice to the necessities which life lays on him. At this time it was specially imperative that the human mind should set to work to discover through science all it could about its environment, in order that it should entrench its species against danger of extinction. Man's response to the necessity must have taken from art a goodly proportion of the creation and the appreciation it had been able to count on in each generation before. So much for the loss on the swings, doubtless made up on the roundabouts, caused by man's brave acceptance of the challenge put to him by the universe. It is not so satisfactory to contemplate the loss caused by his timidity, which thought it wisest to damp down the fires of art, lest his weaker brothers should be terrified by the revelation of what life felt like, and should decide to court that extinction. For such a fear it is that diluted the art of all civilization from the strength of its primitive manifestations. That this fear is base-less, that its pretence to serve the will to live is a mere rationalization of an impulse springing from the will to live, we know when we stand before such rich and sombre works of art as *les pleurants* of Dijon. There is a tradition we feel we must pick up again if we are ever to satisfy a certain hunger. And we know too, as we confront them, that it is the mark of the uncultured upstart to feel that there is anything rootless and revolutionary about those artists of our age, like Lawrence and James Joyce, who want to concern themselves with life in its entirety and death in its awfulness. To those who know the past their special distinction lies in their adherence to the noblest of artistic traditions.

I SHALL not stop again at that inn on the road from Chambéry. Lunch was not good. The French use cooking as a means of self-expression, and this meal perfectly represented the personality of a cook who had spent the morning resting her unwashed chin on the edge of a tureen, pondering whether she should end her life immediately by plunging her head into her abominable soup, or should wreak her spite against the universe by devising one more of her unspeakable repasts. There was trout beside which I felt young and innocent; veal the condition of which was inexplicable unless it had spent its lifetime competing in six-day bicycle races; the spinach was a dark offense. Apart from these culinary malpractices, there was that in the restaurant which gave me a temporary dislike for life. A mean, gross little man, eagerly picking his teeth as out of a general enthusiasm for the decayed detritus of existence,

157

was entertaining a few of his friends to this lunch, a purpose for which it was admirably suited. At the end of the table sat his silent wife, whose body, clad in rusty black, was as much twisted out of the semblance of normal being as an electric standard after a truck has run into it. Somebody asked the horrid little man how he had gained the Legion of Honour that was red in his buttonhole, and he answered, slapping his chest, *"On me l'a donné parceque j'ai fait dix enfants."* The wife continued to eat in silence, her eyes downcast on the plate of loathsome food. Really humanity has come down in the world of late centuries. In the past the Roman Catholic Church urged its flock to increase and multiply, but it did at least attempt to control the quality of that increase by demanding that it should not be heretical, that it should adhere to a certain philosophy which seemed the best available at the time. This method had its obvious defects, but it tended in the right direction. These democracies that call for life no matter of what quality, let all come to them that Mencken wishes.

On the high pass of the Cat's Tooth we stopped
the car and got out, to look down on the Lac de
Bourget. My chauffeur knows it well, having lived
beside it for some of the eleven years he has spent in
France since the war, and he began to tell me how it
takes to itself the bodies of those it drowns and never
gives them back. "Are there currents which drag
them under?" I asked. "No," said he, "it's just bad
water. Can't you see from the colour it's bad water?"
It did, indeed, lie on the landscape like a blue-
green patch of some washable paint rather than a
lake. I rejoiced in the idyllic character of his super-
stition, of which I had already been made aware
from a conversation I had overheard from the
balcony of my villa in the South. "Look!" he had
said, through the darkness, to Jasmine the cook,
"There's a shooting star! What, don't you wish
when you see a shooting star? Why, I've trained

myself so's I wish at the slightest movement, ever since I came down here where there's such a lot of them." My chauffeur was born and reared in a typical modern city of Australia, a land so rationalist that it gives its children a purely secular education; he spent his youth fighting as a gunner in the most scientifically waged war in history, and has since lived by driving automobiles in highly sophisticated parts of the world. It appears, however, that he has the same mystical and animist ideas about the skies above and the waters below as any peasant that lived on a Greek island in the Homeric age.

In TO-DAY's *Continental Daily Mail* I find a paragraph relating to the most popular book of the London summer season, which is the *Life of Lady Byron*, by Ethel Colburn Mayne. Miss Mayne is a distinguished woman of letters who is not so well known in America as she ought to be, for ever since *The Yellow Book* she has been putting out excellent work in the way of short stories, translations, and biographies. The present volume is a pendant to her life of Byron, which is generally admitted to be the best yet written. The paragraph I found did not relate, sad to say, to the conspicuous success and merits of the book. It was such as wrings with sympathy the heart of any fellow author and sends to his lips a prayer that so it may never be with him.

In fact, it was a letter of apology from Miss Mayne, in which she expressed regret for a misstatement she had made. In *The Life of Lady Byron* she had alleged that Marie (the daughter whom Medora Leigh, herself the child of Byron and his half sister Augusta, incestuously conceived by her half sister's husband) changed her name to Ada, lived in Paris in the constant performance of good works, founded the Ada Leigh Homes for Girls, and ultimately married the Archbishop of Ontario. This had struck me when I read it as a most singular example of how even the weariest river may wind somewhere safe to an archiepiscopal see. And alas! it was too singular. Suddenly there appeared before Miss Mayne the angry descendants of the aged but still living Ada and the defunct archbishop, armed with incontrovertible proofs that they were the result not of the confused illicitness of the Byron family but of the ordered legitimacies of various Manchester citizens. The result is this embarrassment for Miss Mayne, and some light on the difficulties of the biographer. For it is inconceivable that she, the most scrupulous of writers, should have committed herself to a statement so bizarre, so likely to be untrue, without receiving what purported to be full verification. In fact, somebody, sometime or other, must have lied.

What a constant war is waged against the possibility of ascertaining the truth by the addiction of the eternal somebody to the pleasures of the lie! I myself received a salutary warning on the subject early in my career, at a time when I was sitting at the feet of a certain English writer, whose indubitable genius made me accept every word he said as gospel. This was unfortunate, for his creativeness cannot bear to let him go free when he stops work, but hands him over to its dark brother, mendacity. In this mood of mistaken credulity I once asked him, knowing that for many years he had been an intimate of Henry James, what the great man's personal life had been while he was conceiving and executing *The Sacred Fount*. For it had seemed to me that this extraordinary interpretation of English social life must have been due to contact with some charming personality, or set of personalities, which had excited Mr. James's always excessive admiration for our aristocracy to a pitch at which he attributed to it graceful and subtle qualities as remote from its original as the Diabelli variations are from theirs.

To my surprise my mentor, usually garrulous, hesitated before he answered, "Well—it was just about that time—but you must never tell anybody— you promise you will never tell anybody?" I promised. "It was about that time," he continued, "that poor Henry had the first of his really bad attacks." "What really bad attacks?" I asked. Over his moony countenance passed that decent and melancholy expression, combined with a peculiar look as if he would like to be able to twitch his ears in some significant direction, which some people wear when they speak of a friend vexed by a certain sort of affliction. *"Oh!"* I breathed, and plucked up my courage later to ask in a hushed voice, "What form did it take?" "Religious mania," he answered shortly. "Poor Henry! . . . Remember, you promised you would never tell anybody. . . ."

I was dumbfounded; and indeed it would have been very interesting if Henry James's nature had revolted against the diet of the secular to which he had restricted himself all his life long and had precipitated him into the most violent kind of those crises which William James (not having so restricted himself) could examine in detachment. "Poor creature!" I said, and, remembering how much he had loved his house at Rye, I asked, "Was he so bad that he had to leave home? Did they have to send him to an asylum?" "No," said my mentor. "They were lucky enough at the very beginning to find a nurse who understood him perfectly. A Miss Gye. Rather a handsome woman, of the Spanish type. You know, heavy down on the upper lip. Oh, I've often met them walking in the streets of Rye. One could see them a long way off, because of her uniform. She wore a shoulder cape of thick blue stuff that showed a scarlet lining when she walked. Whenever I saw that scarlet I used to turn and walk in the opposite direction as quickly as possible. I couldn't bear to see Henry—like that." He relapsed into a silence which I respected. "Funny thing," he said at length, "do you know what soothed Henry more quickly than anything else when he was like that?" I couldn't imagine. "Those ginger biscuits children eat, made in shapes like animals. Give him some of those and he'd be as good as gold. Miss Gye found that out. She was the kind of woman who would."

I went home, and with tears standing in my eyes because of the sufferings of Henry James and the motherliness of Miss Gye, I inscribed in my diary these and many other details my mentor had given me. In the margin I set a solemn note to the effect that these pages were not to be published until it was perfectly certain that no persons whom they might offend still survived. These inscriptions might in time have played the devil with literary history had I not happened, when I was sitting in my mentor's room a week later, to emerge from a reverie saying, "I wonder if Miss Gye could tell us if the lunacy of a genius presents any features that distinguish it from the lunacy of an ordinary man?" To this my mentor disconcertingly replied, "What's that? Who is Miss Gye?" I gaped and said, "Why, Henry James's nurse." Blandly he inquired "Which nurse? Do you mean one of those he had when he was dying?" "Why, no," I stammered. "The one who looked after him when he had religious mania." "When he had religious mania? My dear child!"

exclaimed my astonished mentor. "Who on earth has been filling you up with this stuff? Henry James never had religious mania. He was one of the sanest human beings the world has ever seen!" My gape must have been one of the widest the world has ever seen. "But it was you who told me he had religious mania," I stammered. "Me!" he exclaimed. "My dear child, you're dreaming! Believe me, I never told you any such story, and I should hate it," he added, with something of a heavy-father manner, "to be thought I had ever repeated any such gossip about an old and cherished friend."

I was beyond comment. It did occur to me as a solution of the mystery that perhaps he doubted my discretion and was trying to withdraw the confidence he had made in a moment of rashness. But I was immediately relieved of that idea by the expression on his wife's face as she lifted her eyes from her embroidery and turned on him a prolonged and steady gaze. (They afterwards separated.) It also became charged with sinister import that Gye rhymes with Rye. There is such a thing as rhyme association. Yet who could have failed to believe the tale at the first telling? So much more real than most people is Miss Gye, with the heavy down on her upper lip, her cape with the scarlet lining, and her tender knowledgableness about animal crackers and the afflicted, that she has surely attained a kind of reality. She may not have nursed Henry James

through his bouts of religious mania, but she does
occupy a post as kennel maid on the slopes of the
moon, to tend the chimera, the unicorn, and the
new-born centaurs.

That is the worst of this war between the god of
phantasy and the god of fact, which was not that
which St. Paul spoke of when he said, "In this war
there is no discharge," but might well have been.
The side that cuts its cloth to suit itself can cut it
more in the shape of plausibility. In Chicago,
once, I came across an amateur of letters who was
wedded to the delusion that Mr. Arnold Bennett
had in his hot youth murdered the false friend who
had stolen his mistress from him and had by consequence spent fifteen years in Dartmoor Prison.
The mistake was due to the fascinating conversa-
tional style, at once so elliptical and yet so vivid, so
like first-class tennis, of Mr. Thomas Beer. In describing the life of a literary man who had indeed
thus complicated his early career, Mr. Beer had
served some phrase which had been meant to convey that on this unfortunate's release from prison
he had received some kindness from Mr. Arnold
Bennett; but it had, to the dazzled attention of
his Chicagoan auditor, dropped inches outside the
court. I had the greatest difficulty in putting matters
right and convincing the Chicagoan that Mr. Arnold Bennett comes high in the class (creditably
high, I think we may flatter ourselves) of authors

who can be trusted to leave the death rate as it was; for, as he explained, the extraordinary fervour with which Mr. Bennett writes about ordinary things can only be explained on the hypothesis that the common round acquired an untarnishable glamour for him while he languished in jail. The untrue was the completely credible. Avaunt thee, Miss Gye, wanton sister of Clio! These are two instances when you have been hustled back from the door of literature just in time; but I believe that time after time you have had your will, and we are all deceived.

For some unfathomable reason there are two persons who must never be spoken of candidly in English letters under pain of evoking a hornets' nest of hysterical outcries: one is Byron, the other is Tolstoy. This last loyalty is making the lives of reviewers rather hard just now, since both the earlier and the later *Diaries* of Countess Tolstoy have been brought out, which reveal her husband as a monster of hypocrisy—particularly as to sexual relations, which he denounced publicly as unclean and then exacted not spasmodically but regularly from his wife in a peculiarly unpleasant manner—and of inhuman callousness. "Sonya is suffering as much as ever," he writes cantankerously in his journal only a month after she had buried her favourite son, "and is unable to rise to a religious level. The reason is that she has confused all her spiritual powers with her animal love for her child." And the first loyalty has hit Miss Ethel Colburn Mayne very hard over her book on Lady Byron. Even the *Manchester Guardian*, which we expect to keep its head, published a cold half column declaring that, though the book was well-written, it was unpardonable to write any book on the subject.

This is an odd point of view, especially for Byron's worshippers; for though it shrinks from setting down no detail of his extravagant brutalities to his wife, it ends by showing something very different from the tableau of black angel assaulting white angel which was presented by Harriet Beecher Stowe. It shows, of course, the situation which accounts for Mrs. Stowe's attitude, perhaps the more clearly because Miss Mayne is pre-Strachey in her methods and works not by interpretation but by presentation of the relevant material. There is a superb chapter dealing with the superficially useless and unnecessary interview that took place between Lady Byron and Augusta Leigh, her husband's half sister and mistress, at Reigate in 1851. It is impossible to make out what the two women intended to talk about ("We may not have it in our power, Augusta, to meet again in this life, and to do so might be the means of leaving to both of us a remembrance of deep though sad thankfulness"—and Augusta in as woolly a way "prepared to give and receive any explanations that concerned herself") or what good they could have imagined could have come from such a deferred post-mortem; for it was over a quarter of a century since Byron had died at Missolonghi. Yet when they face each other, and Lady Byron flares up in rage while Augusta huddles in a heap before her, we cannot help but perceive that we have no need to unwind the tangled skein of their argument to find out what they are at. For the moment they are figures of mythic dignity. In the one are incarnated those forces which fight against incest, and will not let life turn in on itself and abandon the task of extending its empire. In the other are incarnated those forces which are all for incest, and inertia, and doing with what one can find on one's own hearthstone, and making as sluggish and easy a passage as may be back to the nothingness whence they came.

But it was not always so. Nothing is more apparent when one has studied the life of Lady Byron than that it was only at moments she incarnated the forces that fight incest, and that those passionate moments had their points of resemblance to the fervid temperance sermons of a preacher who has from time to time known an overwhelming desire to get drunk. Though she was martyred there can be no doubt that she was delivered over to her martyrdom by a strain in herself which though less aggressive than that of Lord Byron was hardly less morbid. Anybody who had a normal reaction to incest would have left Lord Byron at any time throughout that

amazing honeymoon, during which he plainly in-
timated that he was in love with his half sister; and
when he took her to stay with Augusta, and whiled
the long winter evenings away by giving the gross-
est details of his relationship with their hostess and
proudly acknowledging the paternity of her child,
it is hardly credible that a sane woman with a good
home and decent parents should not have retreated
to them. Of course, it is possible that there was a
sentimental explanation for her protracted refusal
to admit to herself that she knew what was being
shouted at her over and over again, and her equally
amazing friendship with Augusta, who seems from
her incoherent correspondence to have been a high-
grade moron. (One of her children was imbecile.)
Lady Byron may have been so infatuated with
Byron that she was determined not to be prised
apart from him until she was hewn off. But such a
degree of infatuation itself requires an explanation.
It is impossible to avoid suspecting that though
Lady Byron consciously accepted the ordinances of
civilization, she unconsciously had the same regres-
sive kink as her husband; and that this conflict between her conscious and her unconscious selves made
her seek out an incestuous situation, thoroughly
embroil herself in it, and then (as she had an extremely well-cultivated conscious self) repudiate it.
    That this is the real reason why she married
Byron, bore her child in such madhouse intimacy

with the deplorable Augusta, and then left him is confirmed by her astonishing behaviour when, thirteen years later, she again came in contact with incest. It horribly happened that Medora Leigh, although still a schoolgirl, was got hold of by her older sister Georgiana, and her sister's husband, Henry Trevanion, a scoundrel of unusual blackness, and induced to become his mistress. The result was that when she was fifteen she was expecting a child. The Trevanions had no money, and the situation was catastrophic. Lady Byron very handsomely came to the rescue with money, but behaved in the oddest way conceivable for a woman who had expressed such loathing of incest. She did not inform Augusta, nor Augusta's husband, Colonel Leigh, who though a ne'er-do-weel had decent enough feelings on these subjects. Simply she supplied funds for Medora to go and have her child at Calais—with the Trevanions.

That was strange. But what was stranger still was that Lady Byron did nothing whatsoever to protect the unfortunate child on her return from France, when, as is piteously reported, she seemed greatly changed and refused to go out in society, "though hitherto she had much enjoyed the public amusements and children's dances to which she had been taken from a very early age." She settled down with her mother, who was still in ignorance of the intrigue, and lived in close association with the Tre-

vanions, in conditions such as made it not surprising
that she should again be expecting a child. In
consequence she eloped with Henry Trevanion (at
Georgiana's instigation) back to France, where she
twice again became a mother before she was twenty
and was subjected to every sort of cruelty at his
hands. Finally she was forced to act as servant to a
new mistress whom he had somehow persuaded to
share the squalor of a ruined château. So the responsibility of having abstained from intervention
was heavy.

It is true that in 1840 she again rescued Medora,
when she was in the last stages of weakness and
misery. But it is significant that she did not do this
till the sexual association between Medora and
Trevanion had been terminated: till, in other words,
she was not interfering with incest. Thereafter the
second cycle followed the same phases as the first.
Lady Byron made the same attempt to establish a
loving intimacy with Medora that she had made
with Augusta, though there was obviously a gulf
between her and the shattered and hysterical girl
which could never be bridged; and in the end she
made the same sweeping gesture of repudiation.
For she showed (and Miss Mayne, strangely enough,
follows her in this) a curious and cruel obtuseness
about Medora's tantrums. She thought Medora
showed wicked ungraciousness and greed because
she would not accept from her an allowance of

fifteen dollars a week for her and her child and in
return give an undertaking to live in seclusion in
France, and because she angrily demanded that her
family should finance her. Yet Medora's attitude
was reasonable enough. Byron had left Augusta a
fortune of half a million dollars, which he had obviously intended for the endowment of Medora. This
inheritance Augusta was frittering away on keeping
her wastrel sons and the abominable Trevanions,
and in fatuous concessions to any blackmailers who
turned up and declared they had "pages from an
interesting diary" or what not. She had once
promised to pay the wretched child a starveling allowance of twelve dollars a week, but had not kept
her word. It was no wonder that Medora screamed
and raged, for she could remember no compensating
kindness on the part of her mother, who, when she
heard that her daughter of sixteen was about to have
a second child, wrote quasi-amorous letters to
Trevanion (whose relations with her before his
marriage were subject to grave suspicion) and with
idiot irrelevance urged Medora to be "prepared by
some clergyman for confirmation at Easter"; and
did no more. Not only was Medora right in her
quarrel with her family, but she was far from being
altogether in the wrong when she fell out with Lady
Byron. She was right in making a fuss because her
allowance was paid through her servants, the
Beaurepaires, for they turned out to be crooks who

in the end blackmailed the Byrons and herself alike. In fixing that allowance Lady Byron showed that exaggerated sense of the usefulness of small sums which is characteristic of the rich. She need not, one feels, have insisted when Medora took a house at Hyères she should furnish a certificate from the mayor that its rent was reasonable; which cannot possibly have been a kind or discreet condition to impose. Throughout there was a curious lack of the sense one would expect any morally sensitive person to have in the circumstances, that nothing could be too much to do to atone to Medora for her desecrated childhood.

Lady Byron must have seen these facts in their true light, since she was both an intelligent and kindly woman, had she not been sealed from clear vision of the external world by preoccupation with an eternal drama of her own. It is noteworthy that all her life she had that difficulty in getting on intimate terms with others which is characteristic of those whose powers are directed inwards to the resolution of a hidden conflict. She was a very friendless woman. It was useless to expect her to respond reasonably to people or events, she was under a compulsion to dramatize her attitude to incest. When one has read Miss Mayne's account of the two relationships through which she did so one can no longer see the Byron marriage as an unequal yoking of saint and devil. Rather does it seem based on a hideous fundamental suitability. Both parties were dominated by the same idea, albeit the husband worked it out in terms of sadism and the wife in terms of masochism. (There was nothing joyful about her repudiation of Medora; it caused her almost as much suffering as her separation from Byron.) Both alike were victims of the crankiness of the human mind, in which primitive ideas may at any time reappear and throw out of gear the apparatus that has been so painfully adapted to civilized uses. Miss Mayne's book confesses an infirmity in man in general rather than brings a charge against Lord Byron. Nobody could possibly object to it save those whose attachment to him is a form of hysteria, an unwholesome fixation on him as a personification of cruelty and abnormality.

How curious are the proceedings of the human mind when it is making these personifications, and how clever in rationalizing themselves into a semblance of being creditable! A considerable part of Byron worship is, of course, sheer perverse adoration of his evil characteristics and hardly troubles to disguise itself. It has provided a considerable body of evidence against itself in the abuse its practitioners have showered on Lady Byron. "She was no better," not the extremest of them said in print, "than any street walker in Piccadilly." A higher sort pretends that what it admires in him is his single-handed stand against social institutions of a cramping kind. Yet nothing is more clear than that he was no such revolutionary. He stood alone in nothing. Though he was sympathetic with the rising of the workmen thrown out of employment by the industrial revolution (his House of Lords speech on the subject is very skilfully used in one of Toller's plays) a study of the Hammonds' book, *The Village Labourer*, will show that there were a great many young men of his class who took the same attitude. Even his regret that Napoleon did not beat Wellington and conquer England had nothing individual about it. Miss Mayne brings out that in this he was following a Whig convention, and that the Whigs used to toast Napoleon at the dinner table. (An echo of this attitude can be caught in Hardy's *The Dynasts*.) Byron at no time during his life in England or in exile showed the slightest discontent with the capitalist system, as Shelley did; and his atheism was nothing like Shelley's proud refusal to bow the knee to something which was unproved and had been used for purposes of oppression. It was, indeed, a superficial affectation often recanted, frequently under stress of that unworthy (because dictated by fear of consequences) brother of contrition known to the Catholic Church as attrition. Even his incest was no unique gesture. It is a practise that constantly springs up in families as mentally diseased as his, and it persisted among the Byrons long after his death, as Medora's story shows. (Henry Trevanion, by the way, was a Byron by blood, as well as by marriage, being a Cornish connection.) In this, as whenever possible, Byron went with a crowd and liked to do so. At the hour which, if the popular account of him were true, should have been his apotheosis, when Lady Byron had left him and the town was up in arms against him, he was utterly crushed and was heard, poor wretch, "weeping in his room."

But that hour, if it proves the hollowness of the invented Byron, proves also what validity there is in the better sort of Byron worship, which takes him as the personification of the Defiance he celebrated in his poetry. That Defiance was, of course, the revolt of the soul against its own development, and the affirmation of its desire to regress and disintegrate. As this is a state into which all human beings fall from time to time, it is not unnatural that they should admire a figure who can personify themselves in that plight, and with such gallantry. For in spite of all Byron's dreary caddishness, his meanness about money, his pert incivilities, and his disloyalties, it does remain true that he bore the tragedy of his temperament with a brave refusal to be daunted by it which absolves him from the final guilt of not fighting for survival.

I said to myself, as I stood on the platform at St. Raphael, that I must buy a book to read on the way up to Paris. To that end I moved back into the station to have a look at the bookstall, but abandoned my intention as soon as I had collided in the doorway with a middle-aged woman. She had something of the stance of a Spanish fighting bull, and I felt a nervous impulse, as I retreated rapidly before her, to make it quite clear that I had never been a matador and had, indeed, always felt a peculiar affection and regard for bulls. Her face suggested the muzzle of a very fierce animal; and her eyes were prolonged by blue lines till the proportion they bore to the rest of her features was queerly non-human. She had taken from her shoulders a wine-coloured scarf of very rich crêpe de Chine to slip through the collar of her bulldog as a lead; and one could believe she would deal as practically with the most precious fabric in the world if there was need.

Nothing I am cataloguing sounds endearing. Yet I forgot about the bookstall, and there was no one in the station who did not watch her and let the pretty girls go hang. It appeared afterwards that it was the novelist, Colette, a personality so strong that for her parallel one has to go outside life to great literature and cite the wife of Bath. In thirty years she has been putting into infallible artistic form her gross, wise, limited, eternal views about life, at times leaving *The Well of Loneliness* beaten at the post, at times producing little candid pearls of innocence, since these too are aspects of the universe. It is one of the peculiar virtues of the French race that it can take the kind of sturdy long-lived strength which in other countries remains dedicated to the body and yoke it to the service of the mind.

SPIRITUALLY I have crawled about on all fours ever since I visited the Cathedral at Aix-en-Provence, and the *gardienne*—a magnificent old lady with the proud face and stiff officious bearing of a pope and a straight back rising from her immense haunches like a wheatsheaf from a field—pointed her several pounds of keys at the tapestries in the choir and announced: "These hung for several hundred years in St. Paul's Cathedral in London." (They didn't. They had come from Canterbury before Wren was born.) *"But of course, when England became pagan, they were sold along with all the other sacred things!"* What a picture of impious ruin! And it held, it imposed itself on the mind. No one could watch her thick white eyebrows meeting in commination without believing that all Northmen were heathen and damned. Also, her tones were weighted with a greater certainty than those who have learned how many-faceted is reality can ever feel. Also, her deep organ notes were such that what she said could not be forgotten. Truth had not half a chance.

In Aix-en-Provence I bought Gide's latest book, *L'Ecole des Femmes*, which Knopf has brought out in translated form on your side, and I read it in bed at Arles, regretting my twelve francs because I see no difference between it and one of the less happy productions of Anne Douglas Sedgwick. There is the same mechanical dodge of showing the reader an intolerable character and then letting another character pass from deluded admiration of it to complete realization of its true nature. These characters are throughout completely static. They collect information about each other and adjust their opinions in consequence, but they do not themselves alter. There is the same difference between this and a real novel in which characters live and develop as there is between straw and grass; but although straw can be put to some good use (though I cannot for the life of me remember what) this dry and un-

necessary exposition of ideas already well established
in the mind of both author and reader before the
book was begun can serve no purpose. All it can do
is to encourage smugness on the part of the reader,
who at the end can say, "Ah! I saw through him
all the time!" The means by which this superfluous
excursus of the mind is made are negative. Neither
the sensuous appearance of this earth without, nor
the conditions of the psychic drama within, are
conveyed by these pages. There is nothing but the
drabbest "he-said-and-she-said" recitation of the
facts (not the essence) of the theme.

Am I showing myself a tasteless ignoramus who
cannot appreciate austerity and subtlety, who does
not understand the beauties of that restrained form,
the *récit?* I will wager that I am not. I know my
Adolphe, and I perceive that in that masterpiece
Constant puts in all that Gide leaves out. It is simple
in its style, but complex enough in its perceptions
and its implications.

"We will leave that book behind," I said in the
morning to my companions, as we were packing.
"It isn't nearly as good as the rest of Gide. . . ."
And immediately I had an uncomfortable recognition that I have used those words nearly every time
I have set down a book by Gide. I might, of course,
have meant that each was worse than the last. But
I had not meant that. I had meant that this book
left a poorer impression on my mind than I had

received on some other occasion from the works of
Gide. I tried, during the next few days, to find out
which particular work had left this richer impression; and I was able to make that search in spite of
the fact that I was travelling through France. At
Nîmes I bought Gide's Essay on Montaigne and
his *L'Immoraliste* to start my course of rereading. I
went over these during the two evenings I spent in
the Cévennes. Then, when I emerged into the
Auvergne, I waited until we got into a decent-sized
town and stopped at one of its several bookshops
and bought some more Gide; and when these were
done I repeated the procedure in another town and
then another. My Gide collection bears the labels of
booksellers in Aix-en-Provence, in Nîmes, in Le
Puy, in Clermont-Ferrand, and in Nevers. Could I,
I wonder, have stopped an automobile at the first
booksellers I saw in Charleston, or Atalanta, or
Nashville, or Lancaster, Pennsylvania, or Troy, and
found a representative collection of the early and
recent works of (let us say) George Moore? I know
that I could not in the equivalent towns in England.
It must be remembered, of course, that there are
two factors which make it possible for a bookseller
in France to carry a large stock, both of which seem
at first sight to carry a hardship that outweighs
their advantage. One is that books are cheap; so
cheap that it is hard to imagine how authors make a
living. Another is that the French public reads

books rather than magazines and journals; and this is in a certain sense a loss, since it leaves the public ill-informed about many facts and controversies of a sort which, happening in England and America, are immediately placed before English and American readers. But these disadvantages are as nothing compared to the awareness of literature this wide diffusion of books brings to the people, and their appreciation of it.

This accounts for many things in French authors: their serene confidence, for one thing, and for another, the ease with which they can make a reputation, and, once the reputation is made, gain acceptance for work that by a less disciplined public would be angrily rejected as not worth the trouble of reading. An English or American author would not do well to bring to market such an unfattened goose as the Essay on Montaigne, which is a patchwork of quotations unified by a commentary directed chiefly to proving, without any startling success, a resemblance between Montaigne and M. Gide. It must be remembered, however, that the French are extremely tolerant of this sort of performance. The essay on "Art and Scholasticism" to which M. Jacques Maritain owes much of his celebrity is just such a compilation, and would in England or America have had little chance of earning respect had it been offered as anything but an undergraduate thesis. Disappointing as this Essay on

Montaigne is, with its attempt to claim robust naturalism on the part of one neither very robust nor very natural, it is yet more inspiriting than *L'Immoraliste*. That I reread one night in a village under the steep chestnut forests of the Cévennes; and in the morning, when I walked up the narrow main street, I wondered if the invention of printing had not in some ways been a mistake. Something seen through an archway caught the eye as imperatively and deliciously as if it had been the jet of a fountain playing in the sunlight; yet there was nothing radiant there, only an exquisite spiral staircase rising from the courtyard of a perfect early sixteenth-century house. My start of appreciation was gloomily transfixed by a suspicion that perhaps man had a more natural turn for stone than for letters. The architects who built this house cannot have been working in very favourable conditions, for this place can never have been anything but a huddling together of poor folks and a halt for benighted travellers. Yet the house was a masterpiece. Stone is recalcitrant stuff. The man who works on it has to keep his mind on the job and cannot run about too much. Better is his case than that of M. Gide, who with a mind adapted to getting the best out of print and finding the phrase that looks well in print, is naturally in touch with all the significant print of his time; and therefore gets caught in a cross draught between the open doors of Dostoievski and

Oscar Wilde, which in this particular case blew him right out of his native land into Africa. In consequence he has produced in *L'Immoraliste* something uncommonly like the earlier works of Robert Hichens. This fee-faw-fum hokum about the man who takes his wife down to the desert, though he knows it will kill her, in order to gratify his appetite for stranger than matrimonial pleasures, is nothing like as poignant a study in the incapacity of the neurotic to feel love as Dreiser's *The American Tragedy*. The surface is better, but that is all.

Next I reread *Les Caves du Vatican*, and I found it, in spite of the magnificent opening, a tame rehash of Dostoievski. The idea of the fraud got up to cheat simple souls into giving up their all by the story that the Pope was being kept a prisoner in the cellars of the Vatican and had to be ransomed is an attempt to fake out of the *donnée* of French life, something like the religious preoccupations and superstitions of Russian folk. The murder committed by the intellectual Lafcadio Wlinuki when he meets in a railway carriage one Amédee Fleurissoire, a simple soul on his way to ransom the Pope, and throws him out on the line for no earthly reason except that he would rather like to commit a murder, is a straight steal from *Crime and Punishment* and *The Possessed*. Gide's enthusiasm for *l'acte gratuit*, the act which is apparently committed for no reason, springs from a morbid determination to deal with Dos-

toievski's material with much less than Dostoievski's penetration and ultimate good sense. Dostoievski knew that slayings and violations are, like
anything else, subject to the law of cause and effect,
and that an apparent *acte gratuit* is merely one whose
motive springs from deeper and more abstract conflicts in the soul than decide the ordinary events of
daily life. Gide's failure to arrive at the same conclusion is due to the error into which his essays on
Dostoievski show him to have fallen. He writes
throughout as if Blake, when he urges mankind to
give itself up to the power of the demon (by which
he means nothing more than the impulsive force in
the mind, of which the reason has not yet been able
to render an exact account), is saying the same thing
as Dostoievski when he declares that man must go
down into the depths of sin and disintegration if he
has to reach the height of holiness and wholeness
through repentance. "This," as Leviticus says
testily, "is confusion." It is a confusion natural
enough for one to make who grew up in a France
dominated by the ideal of "good sense," which at its
best produced Anatole France but at its worst was
responsible for much mechanical pertness of the
sort exhibited by M. Julian Benda, that deplorable
writer so unaccountably recommended by Mr. T. S.
Eliot. But it is a confusion that is certain to invali-
date all thinking based on it.

So far, this rereading of Gide gave me no explanation of his power over the world of letters. But it happened that I found what looked like a clue in a novel of Gide's nearly twenty years old, which I now read for the first time. It is called *Isabelle;* and it seems to me a bad novel, because it bears no relation whatsoever to reality. I am not complaining that it is not realistic, for I have a tender spot for fantasy. But to be tolerable, fantasy, even more than a realistic novel, must have a solid basis in reality, as witness the extraordinarily dreary tales of Hoffmann and his school; and this seems to me to make no correspondences with either the material or the spiritual world. Yet it has a strangely pleasing effect. It has a quality of exquisite softness combined with the most definite memorability, it soothes by its air of familiarity and inevitability at the same time that it excites by its novelty and caprice.

The tale is told by a middle-aged man who, on a country walk with two friends, comes across the ruins of a château, and tells them of the experiences he had there when its walls were still standing. It was then the seat of an old family, and he had gone there to work on a rare manuscript in the library. The place was splendid, but there was a mysterious sense of tragedy and decay about it. The family consisted of an old marquis and his wife, both charming people, and their cousin and his wife, both ridiculous and mentally defective. There is also the marquis's grandchild, a little crippled boy who had to hobble about in irons, and an old abbé who is his tutor. This child's parents were never mentioned directly, but the young scholar discovered a miniature of an exquisitely beautiful girl named Isabelle, who proved to be the marquis's daughter and the un-married mother of the boy. Hidden in a summer-house he found an old letter, which he read with a singularly naïve lack of compunction; and this raised in him a suspicion, which he confirmed by pestering the abbé in a most unguestly fashion, that the girl had been on the point of eloping with a young nobleman of the district when he was killed.

This romantic story, and the beauty of the por-trait, kindled in the young scholar a brooding in-fatuation for Isabelle. He discovered that from time to time she paid nocturnal visits to her unwilling family, and he hung about waiting for one of these occasions. At last she came, and he spied on her from an adjoining room as she interviewed her parents. She was begging for money. Her implora-tions had a tawdry quality. She was in some inde-finable way foul. He understood why the voices of those in the household whom he had persuaded to talk of Isabelle had been heavy with hate, as if they could have accused her of other things as well as crippling her child before its birth by the means she took to hide her pregnancy.

Disillusioned, the young scholar left the château and came back to find that the old marquis and

his wife were dead and Isabelle had come into the
property. She was now living there, superintending
the destruction of her inheritance and conducting
a squalid love affair. He found her sitting in the
park, sewing a new ribbon on a battered old hat,
while she oversaw the workmen who were ruining
the estate by cutting down all the magnificent trees.
He engaged her in conversation, and she in-
advertently betrayed that she was responsible for
her lover's death. For just before the agreed hour of
her elopement she took fright and told an old servant. He was compelled by his duty of protecting the
family honour to lie in wait for the young man and
kill him. Sickened, the young scholar turned his
back on her and left her. Later he comes into money,
and by buying a farm where the crippled boy could
live under the care of this old servant, to whom apparently there attaches no blame, he redeemed the
wrong she had done.

Since this novel consists almost entirely of allegations about its characters unsupported by any
artistic evidence, it may fairly be voted bad. The
reader has a right to expect an answer when he asks
the author, "Why?" He cannot, of course, have a
complete answer, since that could only be given by
an author in possession of the complete truth about
the universe. But he has a right to demand an answer
as complete as humanity's current understanding of
the universe can make it. The author is under an

obligation to analyze his experience in the light of all the other analyses of experience that are accessible to his age, since only if he fulfils this condition can we be sure that art is keeping pace with life instead of falling behind in decadence. But the experience which is the subject of *Isabelle* has hardly been analyzed at all. It is not asking the *récit* to extend its limits if one complains that one is never told (to mention only two unresolved points) what factor in Isabelle's character moves her to turn away from the gracious life of her family to one of sordid and unremunerative gallantries, or what consideration compels the servant to murder the young nobleman instead of merely preventing him from carrying off his mistress. To refer again to the model of this form, *Adolphe*, the author there explains to the reader exactly what factor in Eleonora's character forced her to her miserable existence, and exactly what practical considerations moved Adolphe's father to his various interventions. Because the theme of *Adolphe* is thoroughly worked out in these respects nobody could be left in doubt as to what the theme is: the disposition of certain souls to live for the sake of begetting disharmony instead of harmony. Because *Isabelle* is not thoroughly worked out in these respects one is by no means sure of identifying the theme. Is it that bad women are bad? Since it is not explained how or why they are so, that is hardly a theme.

It fails, obviously, to be an important book when we test it by the standards we are accustomed to apply to works of art. Yet it creates an important effect on the reader; and there can be no doubt at all that Gide is important. It is worth while, therefore, to try it with other tests. If we turn aside from art to fantasy, as it is shown in dream and myth, and keep in mind the observations which have been made on them with a view of discovering what ideas they embody, we instantly find a sense in which *Isabelle* is a success. It is a superb expression of a fantasy, which is recognizable a thousand times elsewhere in folklore and religious belief, in which all evil is attributed to woman. The château is life. It is presided over by two married couples, one of them worthy of respect and affection, the other contemptible and frightening; they are suspiciously like personifications of the two aspects, the reverent and the derided, which the parents assume in the child's eyes. The château would be a place of beauty and virtue, were it not for Isabelle, who is a personification of the sexual aspect of woman. She has crippled her child; that is, she has inflicted on him the pain and humiliation of birth. She cripples him as a result of efforts to appear the virgin she is not; an accusation which expresses the resentment the child feels when it realizes that its mother, whom it has always revered, must have had amorous relations with its father. It is interesting to remember that that arch-neurotic, Byron, repeatedly asserted that his lameness was due to his mother's "false delicacy before his birth," although it is highly improbable that the type of disability from which he suffered could possibly be produced by such a cause, and this not the smallest reason to suspect poor rantipole Mrs. Byron of either true or false delicacy. This wicked woman entraps the young scholar by her portrait, that is, by the romantic simulacrum of herself in which she can make a man believe when she has aroused his passions. When she comes to him in reality she proves to be greedy, she makes demands for money: that is, for strength, for virility. The passage in which the young scholar spies on her as she asks for money curiously resembles folk tales and dreams which on examination prove to depict a child's emotion on realizing that his parents are sexual beings. His dishonourable behaviour in conducting this espionage as well as in reading the letter found in the summerhouse and in sounding the old abbé, reflects the child's sense that in making this discovery it is breaking a command laid on it by an adult world.

In the part of the story that happens after the scholar's return, the denunciation of woman is pursued, more on the score of what she does as a wife than as a mother. There is a suggestion that it is unfair and disastrous that she should inherit the château, which is an expression of the world-wide fear of giving woman power lest they use it to deprive men of their power. The description of Isabelle sitting in the park is full of hatred. The hat is a common symbol for a woman's sex; and the picture of Isabelle tricking out the old battered thing with a fresh gawd is inspired by loathing of the non-virgin woman. The tall tree is a common symbol for a man's sex; and that Isabelle is having them cut down is a dramatization of the fear that sexual relations may be dangerous to men. The secret that Isabelle betrays repeats in compact form the accusation made by the whole scene. She is shown causing the death of her lover. Not content with that, she makes an innocent male, in the person of the old servant, involve himself in the crime; and in that we can see the son's remorse that desire for the mother's attentions should have made him jealous of his father, and his desire to shift the blame onto the woman. When the young scholar turns his back on the abominable woman he is rewarded by becoming rich, and buys safety for the males she has ruined; in other words, he can keep his strength to himself.

To apply these analogies with myth and dream may seem arbitrary; but at least this method does suggest an explanation for the mysterious fact that this demonstrably ineffective novel nevertheless produces an effect. This is not a work of art. It is not an analysis of an experience and a synthesis of the findings into an excitatory complex. It does not have the subjective effect of a work of art; it is not bracing. But it soothes. It repeats a fantasy such as pre-occupied the mind in the days before sound observation of reality could be made; it recalls us to an earlier, and less exacting, stage of our existence, just as a nursery lullaby takes us back to the time when we slept in a cot. Hence its charm, its power to arouse in us a kind of recidivist loyalty, a sluggish gratitude to the book and the author who have led us back from the hard task of being adult.

There, I believe, is the secret of Gide's position. I still refuse to credit that he is a great novelist. I am convinced that he wrote *The Counterfeiters* in the way he did, not because he was experimenting with a new form, but through sheer uncertainty of touch; and that he makes his characters do the many odd things in it, which are never completely explained, not because he is giving a new symbolic account of man's behaviour, but because Dostoievski made his characters behave like that, and he wants to be a great man too. The publication of his journal containing the preliminary notes for *The Counterfeiters* shows him as moved by the most adventitious and uncomprehended forces in deciding the structure of the book. He is grossly imperfect as an artist. His power over his readers lies otherwhere: in his ability to look into his own mind and describe the fantasies that lurk at the bottom of it, the fantasies about life which he conceived as a child and which have determined the whole course of his mental life. This is a very different procedure from that of true greatness. The real giants of the earth record in their work their attempts to test the veracity of their basic fantasies; they turn their attention to those parts of experience to which their fantasies assign importance and try to reëstimate their importance in the light of intellect. If Gide's confinement to a mere record of his fantasies places him far below these giants, it places him far above the dwarfs of this earth. For they put out rationalized restatements of their fantasies, which add nothing to human wisdom but pretend to do so. Since man shrinks from looking at the infantile content of his mind, it is of the highest value that someone should catalogue it. This is Gide's real claim to our respect.

It is not, however, the claim which gives him his hold over his public. We must all feel a certain kinship with Gide as we turn his pages, because the fantasies he reveals are those belonging to the common childhood of the race, and we have all inherited them to some measure. But those who are most thoroughly dominated by these fantasies, who wish to preserve them in their integrity instead of modifying them in consonance with our knowledge of reality, who wish to stay infantile instead of becoming adult, they feel for him a fervent loyalty such as soldiers feel for a general who leads them in

some cause dear to all. Consequently Gide has a
devoted following such as no writer who appealed
to the non-neurotic and the adult could possibly
boast, since those who lead us in the search for reality prefer us to attain independence rather than to
give them worship. He is an index to the neurosis of
contemporary France; and for this reason a certain
phase of his development is of extreme interest.

It is obvious that anyone dominated by the
fantasy which inspires *Isabelle* must come to the
conclusion that since woman is so pernicious man
would be well advised not to love her; and to travel
further to the conclusion that if man has a need
to love and be loved he had better find a lover of his
own sex. From this conclusion Gide did not shrink;
and in *Corydon*, which was at first privately printed
and then publicly issued in 1924, he makes the admission that for many persons homosexuality must
be the easy and obvious course. Now, persons of
old-fashioned views might regard this as a very
shocking admission, which must bring Europe to the
same state of ruin as Rome and Athens; and persons of other views might regard this as the beginning of the Golden Age when, all being free to do
as they may, there shall be no more conflicts, and
harmony shall reign over all. But the subsequent
manifestations of his talents suggest a consequence
that, I think, could have been foreseen by none.

About the same time as he made this admission

an interest in naughty little boys which had been spasmodically visible in his work (notably in *L'Immoraliste*) flowered into an intense preoccupation with criminal children. This came to colossal expression in *The Counterfeiters*, where the young are represented as lecherous, lying, thieving, murderous little monsters; and that this was not a passing phase is shown by the fascinated attention he pays to outrages committed by lads in his occasional commentary in *La Nouvelle Revue Française*. This is seen at once to be a logical phase of his development, if we go back to the *Isabelle* fantasy again. Superficially it is an expression of the hatred felt by man for woman. But previous examination of myth and dream has suggested that such a hatred is too concrete to be an ultimate, that it itself might be an expression of something more abstract. Fantasy has been found to have its basis in a stratum of life lower than that which differentiates between the sexes, but not too low to have shadowy apprehensions of pleasure and punishment, and the sense of guilt. Let us suppose it is not woman who is the fixed object of the man's hatred. That external rôle is played by whatever gives him pleasure. This sense of guilt makes him turn against anything which extends his being by affording him joy. If it be a woman who does this for him, he will (if he is a neurotic) regard her as a criminal and will accuse her; and if it be a youth who does it, he will be treated in the same way. In other words, men who have allowed themselves to be dominated by this fantasy to the extent of fleeing from hetero-sexuality to homosexuality are now going to bring the same charges against youths that they have al-ways brought against women. They are going to allege that they are untrustworthy, dishonest, cold, cruel, and above all, dangerous; and they are going to dwell on, and if need be manufacture, all evidence which supports this thesis. These accusa-tions will be made against children of both sexes, to cover the whole ground of homosexuality.

In this phase of Gide's development his con-temporary quality is manifest. For another author who possesses it to a marked degree, Jean Cocteau, has just published a novel which is full of this fas-cinated and repelled contemplation of children. Any reader who picks up *Les Enfants Terribles*, with-out being aware of the current transference of ac-cusation from women to the young, will find the treatment oddly intense for such a trivial subject. When one had read over a hundred and twenty pages and found nothing but an excited transcrip-tion of the insults exchanged by a schoolboy and his sister in the intervals of indulging in various ado-lescent habits, one becomes puzzled unless one re-members that the author is describing those whom the world in which he lives sees as the source of all pleasure and all sin. This attitude in these authors

cannot be traced to any other than that psychological cause. It would be plausible to suggest as an
alternative explanation that there must be a huge
increase in the number of crimes committed by the
young in France, which, like any other startling
social change, would challenge a novelist's attention. But that increase is in fact trifling, and its lack
of connection with this literary movement can be
judged from the success of Mr. Richard Hughes's
High Wind in Jamaica (the same book as that published in the United States as *The Innocent Voyage*) in
England. For the delinquent child is a rare and not
enterprising figure in English life; and that book far
outdoes *The Counterfeiters* and *Les Enfants Terribles* in
its indictments of childhood.

I have commented in these pages on the dreary
preference of some of the most influential English
critics for novels that resemble tepid cups of sweet-
ened tea. I have now to record the astonishing fact
that these have taken the hot draught of mad
fantasy which Mr. Hughes has offered to them as
if it were one of their favourite cups of tea. It actually owes much of its popularity to the efforts of a
critic who has headed the opposition to Proust on
the ground of his interest in the perverse and unpleasant. Yet in this account of the children who are
captured by pirates and appal them by their cold-
blooded villainy, the book goes to the core of the
embroilment of which poor Proust did but explore

the periphery. It is certain that Mr. Hughes was not conscious of what he was doing, for he could hardly have done it with such magnificent candour if he had. It was of Mr. Hughes that a certain country servant said to her mistress, "A gentleman called when you were out, ma'am, but I didn't know if I ought to let him in, he looked so like Our Lord"; and in the preoccupation with ethereal matters which is reflected in his appearance he probably takes but little notice of the world's changing attitude to morality. His book nevertheless records with a definiteness that has not been surpassed, the new developments in fantasy engendered by the alterations in the situation.

The children on the pirate ship are given the power and the magic of the desired; and they are also given the guilt. It is not true that a little girl of ten would be likely to murder a man for such frivolous reason as made Emily murder the Dutch captain; any more than it is likely that Isabelle would have contrived the murder of her lover, particularly at a moment when it involved her in the blackest tragedy. But pleasure is murderous: if those who give pleasure are to be justly described they must be shown murdering. Those who receive pleasure, on the other hand, are innocent victims: the pirates are shown as gentle and industrious souls whose choice of their career is inexplicable. And there is a gulf between them that is bridged by

no community of substance. The children in the
book are regarded as if they did not belong to the
same species as the grown-ups; just as, in the past,
a great many imaginative works represented men
and women as being two wholly different kinds of
animals. And out of the pages Emily looks with just
the same maddening claim on love and worship, the
same repulsive indifference, as we may see on the
stony faces of goddesses in which primitive man
has recorded his emotions regarding the part
played by women in his universe. In her remoteness
is stated the case that is eternally felt against the
object that gives pleasure: its separateness. For all
its pretence of fusion at the supremest moments of
that pleasure, it does not fuse; and in the moment
when the sense of guilt brings remorse, one cannot
be sure that it is loyally suffering like oneself. Since
obviously man knows nothing more pleasurable than
pleasure, this flaw in pleasure makes his existence
worthless, rewardless.

Beside this statement of Gide's quarrel with the
universe which Mr. Hughes rendered in the con-
sistent and vivid symbolism of poetry, Gide's own
statement of it appears uncertain, full of contra-
dictions, woefully lacking in concentration, and ineffective. His power lies in the steady flow of his
work, all directed to the expression of this current
fantasy, which he has kept up over many years. He
also, with his preoccupations with *l'acte gratuit* and

demons and such-like cullings from Dostoievski, speaks according to the mood of a modern Europe that is eager to learn from Russia what the Roman Catholic Church used to teach it and what it has forgotten since the Reformation. Pascal, though a Catholic, was the true child of a world which even in those parts which did not become Protestant was profoundly affected by Protestantism. He moderated every violence of the spiritual life except depression. But it was a pity to drive out the patristic writers with a fork; since there seems to have been something consonant with reality in their more heightened and extended view of the spiritual life, and humanity is glad when that view is imposed on Europe again through the Russian writers. Coming out of a land where artistic and scientific life are undisciplined by free speech and a free press, these new prophets are foredoomed to extravagance; but Europe takes them and those who use their name, such as Gide. It is certain that he is likely to tell the public ear which has been inclined to him little that is likely to be useful to it. For, as this anti-child movement for which he is responsible shows, his philosophy does nothing to reduce the disharmony of life. There still stands the fundamental ungraciousness whereby those who ought to show kindness to each other in view of favours received spend themselves instead in the devising of cruelties. The only change is in the grouping of persons involved;

and since the grouping of persons exposed to ill-use
and accusation is now composed of those who need
kindness and approbation that they may attain the
best possible maturity, the change is not for the
better.

EVERYWHERE in London just now there are falling leaves. Over in Bloomsbury the plane trees, their branches bare and their creamy trunks half stripped of the brown bark, watch over the wide garden of Grey's Inn like haggard nymphs who have not rags enough to cover their white bodies; and the ravens which ancient custom keeps there, clipping their wings lest they should fly away, huddle dolefully on the coping of the lead cisterns in which the Benchers of the Inn stored water when the Stuarts sat on the throne. "Caw!" say the ravens, and the sounds ask: "Do you feel the earth taking on the substance of a corpse beneath our claws, and the sunlight losing its heat as if it too were dying?" They always ask that question at this time of year.

It is strange that it is to lawyers, devotees of the most arid and artificial of professions, that London owes the glades—such as this and the Middle Temple Garden and Lincoln's Inn Fields, all pleasure grounds belonging to the lawyers' various trade unions—which in the heart of the city preserve the impressionability of nature at its most primitive. They exult and grieve for no other cause than the season of the year, and that with supreme intensity. No public building hung with black streamers on an occasion of national mourning could look so sad as this enclosure, with its trees that drip and drip and drip a tessellation of sad pale gold on the dark lawns, and its ravens corroborating depression on the lip of the leaden cisterns, orange beaks down on black breasts, black ruffs turned up like overcoat collars. Yet there is nothing afoot but the time of the year. It is perhaps one of the most precious advantages of being human that we know winter to be not the end of all things, but the prelude to another spring. We can go out into the country and enjoy the pageant of reddening beeches and the darkening of the fields, without the fear, which all other living creatures must know, that this is the beginning of an eternal dispensation of cold airs, food far to seek, and leafless trees.

This human privilege Virginia Woolf is about to exercise, as we catch sight of her in the street that leads from Grey's Inn Gardens to the Foundling Hospital, standing beside a friend's car, swathing a warm scarf round her shoulders in preparation for a journey. The wind that brings down the autumn leaves must recognize in her a substance nearly as frail as their own when it presses its vigour on her. She braces her austerity against it, turns her back to it, and carries high again her pale, fine face, which unobservant people say is like an old picture. It is not. It is like a very new picture. In fact, I am not sure that it is like any portrait that has yet been painted. In the landscapes of Cézanne and Van Gogh we recognize a quality which comes from a novel and valid way of regarding matter, a manifestation that by following the tradition of art the artists have pushed on into a new phase of sensibility. The distinctive quality of Virginia Woolf's face is that which shows that she has arrived at this phase. It would be fascinating to see a genius of this condition painted by another genius of the same condition. But, alas, the occasions when genius has been painted by genius are few and far between. Perhaps to be great an artist must be so firmly persuaded of the supreme importance of his own medium that eminence in another rank means little to him; and thus neither painter nor sitter seek each other out.

Even as Virginia Woolf braced herself against the wind that blew down the autumn leaves, so she has of late braced herself against an invisible literary wind not less robust and unfriendly. For in *A Room of One's Own* she has, with extreme courage, defied a prevalent fashion among the intelligentsia, which is particularly marked in the case of her admirers. This book (it is really a long essay) is an uncompromising piece of feminist propaganda: I think the ablest yet written. Its main purpose is to defend women from the accusation of inferiority that is laid against them on the ground that they have failed to be geniuses. She proves her case in passages that in their perfect, rounded form, and in the warm yet restrained colour of their imagery, remind one of the great tawny chrysanthemums seen these days in the florists' windows. But make no mistake, she proves her case.

The climax of her eloquence is her biography of an imagined sister of Shakespeare, a genius like himself, who was so frustrated by the restrictions laid on her sex as to physical and mental movement that she died with all her plays still in the unopened packet of her brain. For had she gone to London, Mrs. Woolf very sensibly points out, not hers to hold horses' heads in Southwark and earn without dispute the right to a garret and the production of manuscripts. Hers to be kept hungry by society's reluctance to give the casual jobs to a female, and to be torn asunder by the insistence of man as a whole that she should keep chaste and the insistence of man as an individual that she should not, so that in the end, being with child by Nick Greene, she drowned herself in the Thames. Forcible too is Virginia Woolf's assertion that the belittlement of women's work must have snuffed out many a fiery particle in the way of female genius. For it is the nature of the artist, she admits candidly, to be sensitive to criticism. Nor does she disdain to admit the material handicap laid on women by the different standard of comfort, in certain superb ironical pages chronicling how she fed on partridge and old wine at a men's college at Oxford, and then in a woman's college knew the supreme gastronomic ignominy of prunes and custard. Her argument is inflexible. It is all the more courageous because anti-feminism is so strikingly the correct fashion of the day among the intellectuals.

Before the war conditions were different. The man in the street was anti-feminist, but the writers of quality were pro suffrage. Now the case is reversed. The man in the street accepts the emancipation of women except in some specific instance where he becomes afraid that a woman is doing a man out of a job. But a very large number of the younger male writers adopt an attitude towards women writers which can be deduced from the fact that one of them recently quoted as a right and proper criticism of the intellectual woman the extremely ugly and silly epithet, only interesting as a symptom of his own physical disease, which Baudelaire applied to George Sand. This is due to the rising tide of effeminacy which has been so noticeable since the war. The men who despised us for our specifically female organs chastised us with whips; but those to whom they are a matter for envy chastise us with scorpions.

Now these intellectuals had always made an exception of Virginia Woolf, perhaps because she so obviously is the talent of this generation which is most certain of survival. She had therefore much to lose and nothing to gain by offending their prejudices. These considerations did not make her hold her peace, or blur a single argument. Her honesty is thus shown as remarkable as her sensibility; and that is not the only reason for respecting the author which emerges from this volume. Though she gives herself without stint to the material task of controversy, her temper remains serene. It is as if, advanced beyond the rest of us, she enjoys an extension of our human privilege of seeing a recovery to autumn, and knows that error, like winter, has an end.

SEEING SNAKES

Could it be that the dark agreeable person had said that he was sorry one had not been well lately, and that he hoped one would try playing with the snakes at the Zoo as a means of soothing nerves exacerbated by convalescence? It did not seem to be that sort of a party. But certainly he had said it. He continued to say it, he called for one in an automobile and committed one to what one had meant for purely social assents, not intended to be put into action. And lo! it was true. Playing with snakes is as milk to the nerves. They started one on the smaller sand snakes. "This one," they said, "you'll find very quiet. He's just had a hearty meal of white mice." I ran him through my hands and found him exquisite to handle, a warm, compliant chaplet of repletion. So would I have felt had a god taken me up and run me through his hands, on certain evenings when I have left Foyot's after dining off chicken

en casserole and crêpes suzette. But of the full
pleasure obtainable from snakes I had not experience until I played with one of the large pythons
that trail seven or eight feet along the ground when
they go walking. One picks him up, one passes him
through one's fingers, he gives one back the rhythm
of the movement in a counter movement that curls
him round one's forearm; when one shows him one's
arm can pick up that rhythm too, his reply brings
him above one's elbow; when his head passes above
one's shoulder one offers him the other wrist. He is
a part of one, he is separate from one with a strong
and graceful separateness from which one is proud
to accept whatever rhythm he may lay down.

There is no qualification to one's pleasure, for
there is nothing here repugnant. "It felt like a
snake . . . " Man says that all the world over, and
means the same thing: cold, slimy, fish-like, trailing,
nauseous. And it is not true. A snake feels warm and
dry and clean, exactly as pocketbooks or shoes made
out of snakeskin do. But mankind is full of quaint
errors regarding more important matters than the
sliminess of snakes. We were looking at the huge
reticulated python, that needs sixteen men to
handle it, since it must be kept straight out, lest it
should coil and crush. "How do you give it its
chickens?" I asked the keeper, a lad with a face
round as a butter mushroom. "On a stick," said he,
and added, with a shade of contempt, "it don't

seem to have the *intelligence* to distinguish between my hand and food." What sublime anthropomorphism, to believe that there is a natural division perceptible to all save the dullest eye and mind, between the human hand and that which is appointed to be a python's food! And how universally held it is! Almost as universally held as the belief that a snake, which is warm and dry and clean, is cold and slimy and fish-like.

THE other day a wealthy American who had presented himself at my house just after he had arrived
in England, caught sight of three framed letters that
stand on my mantelpiece. One, as black and white
and neat as winter trees against the sky, ends with
the hope that *vous ne doutiez pas du tendre et respectueux
attachement de votre très humble er très obéissant serviteur,
Voltaire.* The second drives ahead in the large, calm
handwriting that one would never guess to be D. H.
Lawrence's, did one not recall with what serenity he
has kept his unserene course and never deviated into
tameness. The third has its words scratched down
on the paper exquisitely, casually, critically, as if
the writer regarded words as butterflies she had the
power to create, which she a little feared creating,
lest they should attain freedom of flight and do all
manner of things not relevant to the matter reason
has taken in hand. It is inevitable that that should

be the handwriting of Virginia Woolf, the poet whose imagination is so sternly controlled by the critic that she also is. The American expressed envy of these possessions and announced that while he was in England he meant to buy some interesting manuscripts and autographs.

But he spoiled it all by announcing of what authors he meant to acquire these imperishable mementoes. As well could I imagine a sane human being going forth to spend large sums of money in buying up the steering wheels of ancient Fords. Nothing surely can be more obvious than that most of the great names which have dominated the last twenty years stood for something so strictly limited in interest to their own period, and were so loosely connected with the true tradition of art, that to-day they seem like mummy cases. There are, of course, exceptions. George Moore is every year being more and more fully recognized as among the greatest of English writers, and it is inconceivable that he should ever be denied this rank. Shaw and Wells stand below him, but they seem assured of some considerable degree of positive existence. Not so their contemporaries. There are at least two notorious cases where men who in the past seem to have done or to be about to do first-rate work have covered it over with such a plethora of second-rate work that they have lost all critical prestige. The generation that buys their books because it has

heard them referred to respectfully from its youth
up is being succeeded by a generation who will not
buy their books because it regards them as proof
of its parents' bad taste, violently to be rejected.
Why, then, I asked the American, collect mementoes
that will in a decade embarrass the owners as much
as onyx tables or milking stools embarrass the house-
proud wife of to-day?

For, make no mistake, the tin gods have gone
forever. The naturalist novel which was their pride
and glory was a tame and insignificant thing, a
repetition without elucidation, a mere worm cast.
It was English fiction without anything that has
been contributed to it by Defoe, or Fielding, or
Sterne, or Jane Austen, or Scott, or Dickens, or
Thackeray, or Trollope. It had neither wit, nor
passion, nor quick-eyed observation, nor a sense of
the spiritual design that lies beneath the pattern of
material events. It was nearly nothing. When I went
lecturing in the United States (nobody had told
me not to) people asked me if I did not find the
scenery of the Middle West dull. Did I find it dull,
when I had been reviewing English novels for years
upon years? I did not. Therefore, were I an American collector I would have nothing to do with the
manuscripts of the last generation, particularly when
there are writers of the present who are bringing the
English imaginative work back to its tradition and
putting into it its proper dower of wit and passion

and observation and discernment: such as Lawrence, Virginia Woolf, Aldous Huxley, David
Garnett, Stella Benson, the Sitwells, Richard
Hughes. The acquisition of manuscripts by these
hands is not a gamble.

I would even take a risk with the youngest
literary generation of all, and think myself making
a good investment if I bought every manuscript I
could lay hands on by Mr. Evelyn Waugh. This
young man is, I fancy, to be the dazzling figure of
the age as Max Beerbohm was of his. He is in his
early twenties; and in his person he is clear-eyed
and round-cheeked as the cherubim before the
cinquecento got them gross, and as neat as a gar-
denia prepared for the buttonhole. Engaging he is, so
engaging that his literary aspirations would strike one
as pitiful had one not seen any of his performances
and feared the worst on account of his heredity. For
from the point of view of literature his heredity is deplorable. He is the son of Arthur Waugh, a writer
whose fatal impressionability to his own works caused
a tragedy without parallel in the history of letters. In
the 'nineties, when quite a young man, he published
in the *Yellow Book* an essay on "The Necessity for
Reticence in Literature"; and was so convinced by
his own arguments that he thereafter practised the
extremest form of the recommended virtue by never
writing anything else. It is true that he contributed

certain reviews to the *Daily Telegraph*, which used to have a literary page that a weary soul might easily mistake for a four-poster, but even they might be regarded (in their failure to add anything to the matter under discussion) as reticence made positive. Arthur Waugh's elder son, Alec, wrote a remarkable story about English public school life called *The Loom of Youth* when he was still a schoolboy, but he has never since permitted himself to be as interesting as he might be. This is an environment in which the literary burgeoning of the younger son might reasonably be expected to take the form of a quietish essay on Crabbe or a novel about the insipid loves of the immature English. Instead, there was *Decline and Fall*, and now there is *Vile Bodies*.

In *Decline and Fall* Mr. Waugh did what hardly any modern author has done in his first book; he created a character that simply and naturally takes its place among the great characters of fiction that are larger than life-size, and more significant than a single child of man can be. Grimes is one of the world's great rogues, one of those whose serenity and bloomy sense of inner rightness almost persuade honest men that there is a strong moral case for roguery; and he has a subtle value, too, as a vehicle for criticism of our English life. For in him the generation that has spent its youth overshadowed by Dr. Arnold and Rudyard Kipling joyously recognized an embodiment of all the exceedingly queer forms that nature, driven out with a fork from the public school, assumes in order that it may effect a reëntrance. Go to *Journey's End* and look through its sincere and moving emotionalism at the cult of infantilism, the ritualization of all processes likely to lead to insipidity, which sent those men to death children in spite of their age. Then read in *Decline and Fall* the description of Grimes's war experiences, ending in his exquisite thanksgiving to the public-school system: "I've been in the soup pretty often since then, but never quite so badly. Someone always turns up and says, 'I can't see a public school man down and out. Let me put you on your feet again.' I should think," said Grimes, "I've been put on my feet more often than any other living man." Is Mr. Waugh nastily denigrating a fair structure whose fairness gets just rendering in the wholesome mind of Mr. Sherriff? He is not. I admire Mr. Sherriff's talent immensely; and I have no patience with the criticism that cannot keep its mind on æsthetic consideration, and declares that *Journey's End* is a bad play because it is about people whom it is a bore to meet. But I perceive also that he is on a lower plane than Mr. Waugh. If Mr. Sherriff had the power to construct a universe after his own heart, it would probably be a red jam of ennoblement by pain and sacrifice, and so on. But Mr. Waugh's satire—and here he resembles all the best satirists—springs from disappointment of a high hope that there might some day be an end to all that. His ideal universe would maintain itself by harmony; its children would be asked as discipline to refrain from destruction and to win salvation by the invention of new harmonies. It is a nobler dream. In preferring Mr. Waugh's view of public schools to Mr. Sherriff's for this reason, am I being guilty of basing my criticism on other than æsthetic considerations? I do not think so. To be enamoured of the sacrificial conception of salvation is to have a mind so bound to the primal fantasies of man that its work will endlessly repeat and glorify them. Not to be dominated by that obsession is to have a free mind that can look around at reality and proceed without bias to art's proper task of analyzing experience.

There is no Grimes in *Vile Bodies*, and I suppose that humanity will gratify its deep need to be unpleasant by assuring Mr. Waugh that it is not so good as his first book. But it is actually better in many respects. It selects aspects of London and gives amazingly concise and complete renderings of them. There is in London a certain rickety-rackety hotel owned by a lady who cooked for Edward VII and did that and more for the aristocracy of his age, and now trails about all day and all night with a champagne glass in her hand that is always full though she always seems to have emptied it. Time is working on her beauty so that one cannot but think of eternal things, but never was woman so corseted in the temporal things of her particular age. The pale horse is plainly coming soon, but one cannot imagine it save between the shafts of a hansom cab. This peculiar quality of hers, and the fusty and raffish atmosphere of her hotel, Mr. Waugh has perfectly conveyed in a few pages; just as he succeeds, in the chapter about the automobile race, in symbolizing the incoherence which has afflicted society in consequence of the invention of the combustion engine. All these brilliancies are admirably subordinated to the central object of the book, which is to depict the lot befalling youth in modern England. One is reminded of the technique that Anatole France employed when he wanted to give a picture of contemporary France in the Bergeret series. There he hangs side by side panels representing scenes in different houses affected by the political situation that was the real subject of the book; each is a calm, pretty, sunlit, elegant thing, like an eighteenth-century interior, offering a surface of deceptive calm until one looks into it and sees how it marks another stage in the progress of the subject. Mr. Waugh deals with contemporary London in something the same manner, speeding up his tempo to suit our age.

Rather does his technique resemble a card game. His characters fall into the categories of the four suits. There are the spades, the souls doomed to destruction, Miss Agatha Runcible, who spins like a top at parties, round the track at the automobile race, into the nursing home, until she topples over into dementia and death; and the horrid little gossip writer who at last submits to the common consensus of opinion that he is horrible and puts his head into a gas oven. There are the clubs, not so fatal as the spades, but low-priced and fatuous; like the drunken major whose appearances on occasions of public rejoicing give such a dreadful rhythm to the book. There are the diamonds; nobody writing in English has ever conveyed more vindictively the red and swollen appearance that is the badge of those whose success stands for nothing honourable and valid. There are the hearts: Adam and Nina, the two young lovers, in any other age than this inevitably the raw material for romance, in this age forcibly divorced from it. The cards are dealt out, the hands pick themselves up, they play a game, they reshuffle themselves, they play again, till Mr. Waugh's thesis that inspires them has the rubber won as it designed. In the conversations between Adam and Nina, which for tensity rival the best of Hemingway's dialogue, one can see how the designer of the game wishes it were otherwise. Mr. Waugh has the most exquisite sensibility. He has also character. His first book was a monograph on Rossetti which showed great industry, not only in its researches into its subject, but in its groundwork of reading in æsthetics, a subject always distasteful to the lax. Decidedly, I would buy Mr. Evelyn Waugh's manuscripts, were I a collector with an eye to the future.

Those critics who dislike those who were given ten talents in their napkins because they have nothing in their own but holes, often accuse a book of abundance and intricacy as if these were vices: as if an author had no right to demand anything but a minimum of a reader's time and attention. Yet literature is in this matter legitimately entitled to make exactly the same demands as painting and music. If a person standing in front of Botticelli's Birth of Venus should say, "Look here, there are far too many things in this picture. I find it far too great a strain to absorb the whiteness of Venus, and the twining of the two wind spirits in the sky, and the pattern on the robe of the nymph who steps forward to clothe the goddess, and the flowers underfoot and the two stars low on the horizon that are foundering under the inrush of day, and the little bays where it is still nearly night and the water is still dark and cold. The artist ought to have restricted himself to the representation of fewer objects," we should answer, "But you are talking very preposterous nonsense. There are certainly a great many things in this picture, but they are all beautiful things, and if you stand there and look at it in the proper spirit, thanking God for your luck in being able to do so, maybe He will let you see the whole which the painter has made out of all these component parts." If a person should say at a performance of *Don Giovanni*, "I don't like this, the music keeps on changing keys, and it's all broken up into different airs, and you never know where you are because the airs keep on coming back and repeating themselves," we would say coldly, "It is evident that you are not musical. What you say of this performance is simply a melancholy and not interesting record of your own deficiencies." But to any ass who says, "This book is too full of brilliant things and beautiful phrases," or, "I find this book too complicated in its design because its events do not follow the same sequence as in life, and establish relationships that are subtler than those which are commonly the subject of general conversation in a liner smoking room or a women's club party," we extend a tolerance that he does not deserve. It is generally recognized that a picture need not take for its subject an apple on a plate, though some good pictures have done so, and that a sonata need not be written in the key of C major and two-four time and the mood of "Lilla's a Lady," though some good music has dared it. But it is not generally enough recognized that literature need not, neither in treatment nor in subject, be for the tiny tots.

A book cannot be too full of brilliant and beautiful phrases; but somebody may be reading it too quickly to absorb them. A book cannot have too complicated a design if it is significant; but somebody may be too dull witted to comprehend any design more complicated than a triangle. Let such somebodies go and become cooks at Childs and cease to intervene in literary matters. I am not saying that there is no such thing as an over-ornate style; but that has nothing to do with an abundance of beautiful and brilliant phrases; it has to do with an abundance of phrases that cannot be described as beautiful and brilliant since they are not significant and relevant. Neither am I saying that there is no such thing as bad design; but badness of design is far from being the same thing as complication. Ask Botticelli. Ask Bach. Ask Donne or Dante.

THERE is little enough in art that explains and commemorates the love of the sea. The love of sailing in it, yes; but, as Conrad has told us, those who love ships commonly hate the sea. But I am speaking of the true love of the sea, that finds a healing and refreshment not altogether of the body in going down into salt water, that sleeps better if the house is within earshot of the rocking tides, that thinks green, blue, and grey, if they be but glassy and edged with foam, the best of all colours. There are of course endless sentimental novels in which the hero or heroine grows up beside the sea, regards it as a kind of wild aunt, leaves it to go to the great city, is there disillusioned by the heartless behaviour of sir or madam as the case may be, and comes back to die on the shore, usually to the accompaniment of a great storm. But these are lewd tropes of the anthropomorphic fancy; the genuine faculty of the imagination has very rarely been exercised on the subject. So there was the charm of the unusual as well as of the beautiful about the statue of Venus arising from the foam which young Maurice Lambert showed in his exhibition at Arthur Tooth's gallery. With Brancusi-like courage he has taken away from her not only the head and arms but also the shoulders, so there is nothing to her but a gleaming, rounded slimness, slithering as things are that come out of the waves. In fact, she is made of cast iron, but the moulding of her planes convert her to the substance of a mermaid, which is nearly the substance of a fish.

There is about this statue, as about all Maurice Lambert's sculpture, a beautiful "cut-back" quality. The design has everything pruned away from it that might tend not only to extravagance, but to the too easy realization of its purpose. This characteristic is typically manifested in a group of alabaster birds. It is as if Maurice Lambert had said to himself, "I believe that an arrangement of masses in certain relations to one another will express the experience of seeing a flight of birds rising from the ground. If I am right, then that arrangement will do it in its most self-contained terms. I will not have my conception recommended to the spectator's attention by prolongation of the masses that will remind them not of birds—my arrangement will do that all right—but of the hackneyed representations of birds to which they are accustomed. So here goes, as purely itself as I can make it." The conception stands the test; and here and in a dozen other grounds, honesty and restraint working in collaboration with a strong and ambitious imagination make a promise of greatness.

Maurice Lambert is not yet thirty. Constant, his brother, is twenty-five years old and stands as high as a composer as his brother does as a sculptor. It is curious to trace a family resemblance in their work, different as the medium is. The other night I went to a concert at Queen's Hall to hear him conduct his setting of Sacheverell Sitwell's poem "Rio Grande," which is considered as important a musical production as this isle has seen for some time. It was preluded by Beethoven's Eroica Symphony. Many a minor conductor and many a listener has tried to lend a martial quality to this work because of its name and its dedication to Napoleon, since they did not know that Beethoven wrote it when he believed that Napoleon was about to give France and the world a new constitution based on Plato's Republic. That error was avoided on this occasion, and the performance was excellent. There followed, however, a deplorable piano concerto by Tschaikowsky, full of lax prettiness, and to while the time away I read the programme. There I unfortunately came on Wagner's notes on the Eroica Symphony, and found that this was one of the occasions when it is better to listen than to look, though I was so fascinated by horror that I could not desist. The hero of Beethoven's music, who came to impose order on the chaotic phenomena of life, embodied in "the manlike principal theme, striding sturdily through all the piece," to whom comes "the womanly, which reveals itself in ever more intense, more many-sided sympathy, as the overwhelming power of *love*." It was repugnant beyond words. The contrast between Beethoven's music and Tschaikowsky's, and the tune of this commentary, made one feel that during the last hundred years the world has been overgrown with large spongy fungoid growths of emotion. But then Constant Lambert came on the platform and set to work dominating the choir and orchestra with the tremendous liveliness of his compact gladiatorial figure. He is one of those who shine so brightly with their own vitality that one's weatherbeaten intelligence, having learned so often that all that glitters is not gold, prepares for disappointment, but here pessimism is as foolish as optimism usually is.

The sounds came right. This was music much nearer Beethoven than the Tschaikowsky piano concerto; it was written by somebody not persuaded, as Wagner was, of the artistic propriety of being abandoned to emotion. There was here the same beautiful "cut-back" quality that there is in Maurice Lambert's sculpture. He says to himself, "I believe that an arrangement of sounds in certain relations to one another will express the experience of reading Sacheverell Sitwell's poem and exposing one's imagination to its suggestions of a baroque city. If I am right, that arrangement will do it in its most self-contained terms. I will not have my conception recommended to the audience's attention by any resort to familiar tunes and rhythms that are associated in the listeners' minds with this kind of theme. So here goes, as purely itself as I can make it." There, too, is a convincing promise of greatness.

THE other day, at the Théâtre des Arts in Paris, I saw a play by Brückner (the mystery German or Austrian author whom nobody knows) called in its French dress *Les Criminels*. It has been running for two years in Berlin, I am told; and the heart is bowed down by the thought that for all that time a community should have let itself listen to such jackassery. Its superbly simple thesis is that the law operates in such a way that all the innocent automatically go to jail and all the guilty automatically stay out of it. Now, God knows that jail is a cruel place, and those that languish there deserve our prayers rather than our blame; but really that is not all there is to the law. The critics and audiences who swallow this kind of thing presumably never learnt anything at school about Justinian and the foundation he laid for modern civilization by his codification of the law, and the declaration he made that the jungle days were over and done with by his nice consideration of the laws regarding slavery and debt. They had apparently never excited their adolescence by reading the correspondence between Thibaut and Savigny, in which the Romanticist follower of Rousseau cried out for a code based on the principles of Natural Law, and the hard-headed historian proved that laws grow organically out of social conditions, and that the legislator's task is to adapt legal tradition to the needs of the present. I recognize in Brückner's play an inconsistency which, here as in Galsworthy's plays inspired by the same heresy, tortures one's need for intellectual honesty. The author tries to eat his cake and have it too. He assumed determinism in the case of the persecuted, so that he need not blame them for what faults they commit in the cause of persecution. In other words, he is a sentimentalist; what he cares for is not discovering the truth about his material but creating with it the greatest possible emotional effect on the audience.

But in *Les Criminels*, like two masterpieces in a provincial museum full of rubbish, are the Pitoeffs. The play uses the technique of *Street Scene* and shows an apartment house with a transparent wall. Most of the rooms are filled with epicene innocents and lugubrious infanticides, but there are also visible a waiter, and a cook. The waiter is a miserable fellow, not even a restaurant waiter, a café waiter; but nevertheless he is a beauty man, one of those who can by a leer and a smack cause such dreams in the female as might be engendered if a god had smiled and caressed. He seduces the cook, for no other reason than that she happens to be in the room at the time. But he has another mistress, a plump and blowsy wench who runs a bar in the same house, who is very well suited to him. In a scene where she goes to her cupboard after an encounter with him and takes out her money bag there is a simplicity that stops the heart in her giving and his taking. One seems to look down an immense long vista to a vanishing point where there is no more romanticism, no more of anything that can be expressed by an abstract noun: nothing but a thing in itself . . . What thing? The bare minimum of the recognition of reality to which the organism can restrict itself and go on living. This recognition is the deliberate choice of minds that want to wallow. The waiter and the wench had the vitality to soar to the romantic had they desired. Rather are they children of a race that, wandering long on the feculent soil of this globe, have become convinced of the futility of aspiration and are content to squat. They belong, in fact, to the family of Leopold Bloom.

But the cook belongs to that more foolish family that persists in soaring. She (played by Ludmilla Pitoeff) is a Gothic Madonna; at times oddly reminiscent of a certain dance by Angna Enters. When she finds out that her lover has been false to her with this trull she immediately strangles him. But not, it must be marked, out of jealousy: out of a philosophical fanaticism. She is enraged by the infidelity because it proves the parties involved to be the kind of person which is the natural enemy of her kind of person. She will not believe that love is what these others say it is, that life ought to be what they make it. With as noble an intention as any mediæval Christian that martyred a Jew, or any Mahommedan that stones a Hindu in an Indian riot, she brings them both to death. For as coldly as she kills the wench, she lets the waiter be arrested for the crime. Even she bears witness against him. Steadily implacable, she will not lift her finger to save him when he is condemned to die, she will not sign a petition for his reprieve. These two have committed the sin against the Holy Ghost by rejecting love; thereby they destroyed with their minds a part of God's creation. For that great sin they must pay the supreme penalty.

Their positions are defined with diagrammatic clearness in the court scene. The waiter sits in the dock facing this occasion, as he and his kind have agreed that all occasions in life should be faced, with grins and shrugs. The cook come to bear witness against him stands straight and pure like a sculptured figure from Chartres or Vézelay. There is one superb moment when the judge inquires, as judges are apt to do, with an irrelevance that is near to naughtiness, into certain sexual aspects of the judged events. He drags into prominence some hypothetical matter regarding progeny. "No," says the cook, "he did not give me a child." The icy kind of hatred congeals her tones. "But perhaps that was his fault. He hasn't got any children." Even so did the righteously enraged inhabitants of invaded Ireland accuse Cromwell's soldiers of tossing infants on pikes; even so did the Belgian refugees accuse the Uhlans of nailing ten-year-old boys to barn doors with their bayonets; not because they had seen these things, but on the grounds that since their enemies had done so much, this crime also they had probably committed. He had offended against the romantic theories of which her lost virginity had been the symbol. It would, therefore, not surprise her did he offend against the service of life of which her unachieved motherhood was the symbol. But he does not take it as she meant it. *"Pas si bête,"* he guffaws, construing it as a neat thrust in the kind of verbal rough-and-tumble that is apt to succeed sexual engagements, and no harm done. His genial readiness to let her score her point, the good fellowship with which he leans from the dock and tries to wheedle her back to him with a pet name, shows that in his infidelity to her there had been no ill-will. His ill-will was only against love, his real adulterous preference was for the leer as against the smile.

So far outside his world are any ideas of guilt or atonement that it never occurs to him that she is bearing false witness against him. Murder is off his beat, like love and all other matters of high tension. But justice takes its course, and he is condemned to death. When he hears his sentence he makes a gesture that lives in my memory as the richest in imaginative implications I have seen on the stage. For a minute he sits still. By his attitude he makes one see Death like a vast black cavern yawning in front of him. Suddenly he realizes his danger, recognizes that this cave is going to swallow him, and organizes the spry body which has carried so many trays and leaped upon so many ladies to meet this occasion also. He springs up and lifts the stool he has been sitting on high over his head, as if he were coping with a café brawl. His soul protests that there is nothing in the universe as grave as death now appears, that everything is no more and no less important than a café brawl. In this terrific movement which in a twinkling contracts the composition formed by the actor from something covering the whole stage and diminishes it to the short vertical line of himself and the stool, this argument is stated with a force which prints it on the air for the rest of the play. He does not appear again, but this image lingers to give ironic point to the further unfolding of the cook's so different argument. Even as all the parts of a church, transept, nave, chapel and choir, ambulatory, crypt, are dominated by an altar and other references to the atonement, so all the workings of her mind lead her back to ideas of guilt and sacrifice. She has done vengeance on those who rejected the Lord's creation, and that was right. But vengeance is the Lord's and must not be usurped. Therefore now it is just that she herself should perish. She takes poison; and as she does so she becomes like one of those Madonnas who gather into their hearts a sheaf of swords. Her argument is as perfectly stated as was his. Two aspects of humanity which now we envisage chiefly in terms of abstract thought are clothed with flesh as if we lived in the Golden Age and man could incarnate each type of his own being as a god and send it off to live an independent life on Olympus. The Pitoeffs make all other theatrical performances seem thin and limited, on a poorer level of being, just because they seem to possess this primitive power of creation, together with the power of critical thought, which in their case coöperate instead of being mutually destructive. They kill the old idea that a good actor must have no intellect.

At the Comédie des Champs Elysées there was *Amphitryon 38*, a flat-footed mythological comedy on the subject of Jupiter's love for Alcmena, the wife of Amphitryon, by Jean Giraudoux, who seems to me (and I fancy to most English and American playgoers) as boring as a dramatist as he is entertaining as a novelist. *Bella* was superbly contemporary. I am willing to admit that he cannot see an inch below the surface, but what a clear and comprehensive vision he has of that surface! The picture he gives of the Bertholet and the Poincaré families gratifying the Jehovah complex of their race by interpenetrating the natural life of France with their dry, efficient, all-embracing activities would be more honoured if he had given his book the right masterpiece look by making it slightly dull. For it was superbly done, particularly in the rendering of the cynical attitude of the younger generation which (since Jehovah insists on eternity as a working tradition) reduces to naught the labours of their elders. But the value of such snapshots depends entirely on the rarity of the subject. If many other photographs of it exists, some of them carefully taken under studio conditions, there is no point in the sketch in commemoration. Of the changing externalities of life there is never an amplitude of leisured record; those who are in possession of information regarding them are too busy acquiring it to be artists. For that reason the snapshots of politics in *Bella* are beyond price. But of the constantly recurrent events of the heart there are now a multitude of records. Therefore there is no special value in *Amphitryon 38*, which is a series of snapshots of the crisis produced when Jupiter fell in love with a woman who, adoring her husband, had no use for a divine lover, and begged off. It has the extreme superfluity of a tourist's snapshot of the Taj Mahal.

Yet it is worth seeing the play just for the performance given by the actress who plays Alcmena. Valentine Tessier is a glorious beauty. She has red-gold hair that seems to have learned how to grow from a sculptor; vast dark blue eyes, not insipid but like the sea; a mouth and chin that have something of the melting and mischievous conformation of Ellen Terry's; when she walks she rides space in the manner of the Winged Victory. Most French actresses have an air of having been born of a tired soubrette in the wings of the second best theatre in Lyons and of having arrived at maturity by expedients that leave one reflecting that it takes all sorts of circumstances to make an orchid, but Valentine Tessier is plainly pellucid in all things, even to her origins. I have never understood what exactly Shakespeare meant when he used the phrase "inland bred" to describe those who are lettered and have manners, but I am certain that Mlle Tessier is "inland bred." She is intelligent too. Not a poor little point in the script but that she launched on the rich flood of her voice and gave its chance to make its voyage. She is one of the most delicious of human beings; yet hardly at all did she mitigate the ultimate tedium of the evening. Why was this? Because her performance was the equivalent in the theatre of a purely representational painting, of an old-fashioned naturalist novel. She gave an exact imitation of the behaviour of a virtuous woman in the given circumstances. There is nothing here stylized. There never comes the gesture, or the intonation, that are relevant not to the actual lines spoken, and to the movement dictated by the script, but to the philosophical conception which the play and the part should arouse in the audience's mind. One simply said to oneself, "This woman makes every single separate moment very agreeable. If I were a man I should long to marry her. She would spin out life into a sequence of delights." But there is required for art the very reverse of this motion: which shall contract all moments of a lifetime into three hours, so that the pattern of life can be clearly discerned.

O<small>NE</small> had to go to the Théâtre Pigalle because of its claims to be the most modern theatre in the world. So it is, and grandly. It has an entrance hall that makes a new kind of magnificence by having in the middle, as a balustrade to a staircase and upper landing, a wall of horizontal aluminum bars on which lights are trained, so that columns of brightness appear in various positions as one walks about; so that one is faced with a moving architectural composition, the main features of which are intangible. It has also an underground picture gallery, very seemly in its proportions, where they have art exhibitions of the first importance which are to be visited during the entr'actes. This is shocking as all attempts—such as the playing of really good music in the entr'actes—to seduce the attention into polygamous relations with more than one art at a time. The Théâtre Pigalle, however, is but one more il-

lustration of the sad fact that on the stage the most
elaborate envelopes often contain the briefest and
most jejune messages. For they were playing a
tragedy by Lenormand called *Le Simoon,* which
was no worse and no better than *White Cargo,* being
just that sad tale of heat and Imperialist responsibility laid in French Africa.

Its chief interest was the hint it threw out that the
arts of a country may be mutually destructive. The
theme of the play is the calamitous fate of a French
Colonial administrator in Algeria who is living with
a savage half-caste mistress, when his wife dies
and his young daughter is sent out to him straight
from a convent. He forms an incestuous passion for
his daughter, who flies in horror from him to the arms
of a practising sheikh, but is waylaid and murdered
on the way by the half-caste mistress, who wants
the sheikh for herself. It might have been possible
for Lenormand to establish these facts in the world
of imagination had it not also been true that cooking
is among the greatest of French arts. Mushroom
omelettes, chicken done in cream with truffles,
crêpes suzette had laid inches on the hips of the
half-caste mistress. They had also implanted a deep
peace in her soul, a proper sense of values, that forbade her stabbing her lover's daughter with anything like the proper conviction. Would one do that
for a sheikh when there is still potage St. Germaine?
Gémier is a great actor, his voice and movements are

papal in their authority. But even so, the greatness
of his country in this other art had done that to his
figure which impeded his greatness past argument.
As he laboured to convey the workings of incestuous lust he looked remarkably like Father after he
has been mowing the lawn on a hot afternoon.

In these circumstances the play found it hard to
get its way; though it was not so utterly worsted as
The Shanghai Gesture, when I saw it a night or two
later. I strayed to it because when I saw it in New
York it struck me as infinitely the best melodrama
I had ever seen; and I wanted to see how Jane
Marnac, a sleek creature who is a star simply because from her youth up she has always got the
front seat, would handle a part that in the hands of
Florence Reed had provoked a display of action as
prodigious as an oil gush but made curiously un-
glamorous by its professionalism. "I am able to do
this because I have been acting for years," she
seemed to be saying. "Lord! One learns a lot in
these stock companies! I've put over dozens of bad
plays in my time, and I suppose I shall put over
dozens more before I'm done." Here was incredulity
that the front seat could ever be attained.

But my curiosity as to the behaviour of con-
trasted types in similar circumstances was, as it happened, not to be gratified. Jane Marnac was ab-
sent, and Madame God-dam was in the hands of an
understudy, a dark, squarish, dutiful-looking woman

of the type represented in Ruth Suckow's more poignant studies of repression. The poor lady's difficulties in adapting herself to the part were increased by the circumstance that she had been given no time to learn her words. From the second act most of her lines were given to her first by the prompter, then, as she was too flustered to take them from him, by other members of the cast, and lastly, with cruel hilarity, by the audience. *"Il faut que je te tue,"* hissed the prompter, *"Il faut que je te tue, il faut que je te tue,"* came from various quarters of the stage, and *"Il faut quevous la tuez,"* mocked the stalls. But it was French cooking that gave the play its death blow. The great thrill of the play comes in the last act when Florence Reed used to pursue Mary Duncan first up and then over and down the double staircase outside Madame God-dam's establishment, catching her up and stripping her half-naked just before she got her to the ground and killed her. That staircase, however, never came into play in Paris. When the time came for the pursuit, mother and daughter looked at it over their shoulders in an embarrassed manner. Mushroom omelettes, chicken done with truffles and cream, crêpes suzette, the beneficent action of these on both parties would have prevented any chase they might have started up that staircase from ranking as a sporting event. Moreover, timber would have learned its limitations. They settled their differences on the level, with such a marked diminution of the dramatic effect that when the curtain fell the audience remained seated, though the circumstance that they could have hoped anything more would happen to the dramatis personæ cast a lurid light on their home lives.

Their hilarity at the plight of the unfortunate understudy was definitely cruel. Yet the cruelty of the French I find not altogether unforgivable. Unless France had sheathed its nerves in callousness it could hardly have proceeded with its business of creating a civilization in the face of constant agonizing interruptions imposed on it by its wars and the internal disorders caused by its political and administrative incompetence. Also it had had to steel itself against its own poverty. There is no unemployment in France. But on what incredible wages do the employed exist! The other day I visited a famous French scientific institute and found that the laboratory assistants (not graduates, of course, but serious craftsmen) were paid from six to eight hundred francs a month, and they thought themselves not ill-rewarded in contrast with their fellows. That which enables man to endure has a special value in this community, whether its moral face is fair or not. Hence, at the Casino de Paris, the admired presence of Mistinguette.

She is said to be sixty-four, and though the malice of man may have set the calculation a few years out, it is certainly true that in a few years or so she will be

a grand old peasant woman. She looks as if decade
after decade she had tackled her food with an iron
digestion, and elbowed her way to the front whenever it was good to be there and stayed like a rock
at the back when that was the better place. "Mere
beauty is all very well," say the audience ecstati-
cally, "but this, this is an ideal." The presentation
of that ideal is not without its humours. Mistinguette
has kept her beautiful legs, but her torso has
thickened with age. This, since she brooks no compe-
tition from the female chorus, leads to a convention
not usual in a revue. There is in one scene a wind
coming up from the boards which blows up the
skirts of all parties concerned and shows their legs,
to Mistinguette's honour and glory. But the other
parts of the body have to be kept covered lest she be
worsted. With a few exceptions the chorus remained
swaddled to the chin in its winter woollies. Superb
manœuvre! So one can imagine some old woman
sublimating her rage at the fact that the best
pasturage near her cottage belongs not to her but to
her neighbour, by contriving that after dark, at
least, her geese sometimes feed there all the same.
Enraptured, the audience tells stories of the incredible economies of "Miss." It all explains how France
has survived the Bourbons, the Buonapartes, the
Quai d'Orsai.

In the theatre it has often been proved that if one lets an actress play leading rôles long enough she is quite likely to learn how to act. In France there has arisen a playwright who has proved that if one lets an author write popular successes long enough he will in time learn how to write a play. For surely Bourdet's *La Prisonnière* was a dull, made play of the old-fashioned Pinero type. His success with that, however, made him sit down at his desk in a more light-hearted mood, and he achieved *Vient de Paraître*, a delightful comedy. It was translated into English by Mr. Somerset Maugham and Mr. Gerald Haxton, but has not been produced in either London or New York, though it certainly should do well in New York. For it deals with complications introduced into French literary life by the award of such prizes as the Goncourt and the Femina, which are not so unlike the complications introduced

into American literary life by the book-buying
clubs. The resemblance is not complete, for I cannot
see an American publisher, wearied by an author's
failure to follow up a success he had initiated by
being honoured by the Literary Guild or the Book
of the Month Club, attempting to stimulate his
imagination by arranging romantic entanglements.
Not thus, surely, will Messrs. Simon and Schuster
handle Aloysius Horn.

But though *Vient de Paraître* was all right, it was
not grandly so. There Bourdet exposed the vanity
and callousness of the artist not merely to raise a
laugh but to ask himself the question which many
a saint has asked, "If the effect of increasing self-
consciousness is to make man criticize out of existence so many of his impulses that previously resulted in benevolent action, had we not better stay
vegetables?" But he observed the formulation of it,
and indefinitely postponed an answer to it by indulging in pretty sentimentalities. Now he asks
himself a question not so easy to formulate in words
yet clearly enough formulable by the persons of his
comedy *Le Sexe Faible*. He takes one of those French
families that no longer worry about securing good
marriages for their daughters—it is too difficult,
and anyway the girls prove to be admirably able to
fend for themselves in business—but now try to
marry off their sons to heiresses from the United
States or South America. He represents the family

as living in a palace plainly recognizable as the Ritz, and as having their affairs controlled by the head waiter, M. Antoine, who is as plainly recognizable as M. Ollivier, the head waiter of the Ritz. This character is beautifully played by Victor Boucher, an exquisite actor, bland as sauce Béchamel, yet infinitely expressive. Mildly he seems to be asking Heaven what a just man should do if he is born to the office of Pandarus, and to be patting down the grave of hope because no answer comes, yet not losing his serenity. He stands there, silently mourning for ancient decency, but politely aiding modern indecency, while the flux of a world in which all the men play the part of women and all the women play the part of men boils and bubbles round him.

Superb is Antoine in his melancholy conversation with a Russian countess who goes up and down the hotel corridors seeking for personable young men with all the allure of a shark. Even more superb is he in his scenes with Carlos, a South American gigolo, who is played with something like genius by a youngster called José Noguero. Because of his name it has been supposed that he is simply a South American behaving on the stage according to his natural bent; but in actual fact he is a Bordelais of Spanish origin, and this is a real impersonation. It begins with the assumption of an accent, and a tight and doggish cut of tailoring, but it does not

end there. All the spiritual determinants and pre-
dicaments of a gigolo's life are here defined. The
mixture of mercenary expectation and romantic
hope which make him as they make the courtesan
is made visible to us in the scene where the head
waiter, dutifully anxious to oblige a young woman
who is among his favoured clients and has made
enough out of her dressmaking house to adopt a
male attitude to her pleasures, flashes a diamond
ring before Carlos's eyes. The gigolo's eyes, dark,
oily, base, yet indubitably full of passion, shining
like the foul but starlit waters of a tropical port,
roll round and round as they follow the white
stones, fascinated half by their brilliance and half by
their value. The penalties inflicted by society on this
pliant and confused type is presented in the scene
where, huddled in his chair, he cries, "Why will nobody marry me? These American women always
say they will marry me, and they never do," and M.
Antoine answers: "Ah, Monsieur Carlos, you have
allowed them to discover that they can enjoy your
favours without going to the trouble of marriage.
When that is known about a young man there is
very little hope for him. If I were you I would seek
my fortunes in the provinces." A slight complacence
tinges his tone, as of a matron who is broad-minded
in her attitude to those who are not as she is, but
cannot refrain from feeling that a little credit at-

taches to her for getting on the right side of the fence; and nothing could be more Magdalenish than the dejected pose of Carlos. The younger Dumas must turn in his grave as they play each night this play which might as aptly have been called *Le Monsieur aux Camélias*.

IT IS difficult to describe accurately the effect that
D. H. Lawrence's death had on London. If one
says that the effect was tremendous, one makes a
suggestion of a capital in mourning, which is
ludicrous. Not even among his own caste was he
honoured as he should have been. I myself realized
with a shock how much of what I had always put
down as Lawrence's persecution mania had a solid
basis, in fact, when I read obituaries in which not
only was the homage due from the living to dead
genius meanly denied, but the courtesy paid to
any corpse was so far as possible withheld. "Messy
stuff," was the delicate phrase bestowed by one of
our greatest dailies on his poetry. He might, judging
from another of them, have been a lunatic of the
same sort as those who, though normal and even
exceptionally gifted at most times, every now and

257

then embarrass their friends by suddenly removing their clothes in public places. Less crass than these but just as infuriating were the articles by mediocrities whom we cannot blame for having stayed in safety, since they plainly lacked the vitality to push on the long journey to the edge of danger. They made excuses for Lawrence. It appeared to them that he saw life as a flaming mystery because he suffered from tuberculosis, though nothing seemed plainer to those who knew him best than that this malady gained its hold only because his intense perceptions had exhausted his body. It appeared to them that he wanted to crack the crust which society has allowed to form on the surface of its existence and look underneath, because he was a miner's son and had an inferiority complex about the respectable. If that were true, it were still not to be sneered at, for if a creature of such quality as Lawrence found himself in a world that by its social ordinances ignored that quality, he had a right to question those ordinances. But there was so much more than that in the spiritual drama of Lawrence's life that it is not true. Those traits in Lawrence could hardly have emerged save to those who were regarding their subject very oddly because they were looking at it through the wrong end of field glasses, wishing to see that which is much greater than themselves as much less.

The most sympathetic obituary I have yet seen

was an affectionate note on him as a man which appeared in the *Times* Literary Supplement.

I desire (if I can) [says the anonymous writer] to correct the impression, which is widespread, that D. H. Lawrence was a madman of genius, savagely bent on violating sanctuaries, and bruising the finer conscience of his fellow men. To defend Lawrence's passionate convictions is no part of my hasty undertaking. These do not need to be defended, only to be understood, and understood in the light of an experience extraordinary in its depths and comprehensiveness. And again I am not invoking the beauty of his personality to excuse his work. It is right that I should make it clear that I do not consider his work needs any excuse.

It is true that the unknown goes on to say:

If it was wrong, it was passionately wrong; and to be passionately wrong is far better than to be coldly right,

a sentence which I find it impossible to record without expressing my dissent.

If it was not right, it was not right with attendant conditions that have no demonstrable connection with values, and to be not right with these attendant conditions that have no demonstrable connection with values is to be more right than to be right with other attendant conditions that also have no demonstrable connection with values.

Such a statement seems to me wrong in itself, and unnecessary as a defence of Lawrence, since he was passionately right. But we can follow this anonymous writer without question when he says:

> Lawrence was the most remarkable and the most lovable man I have ever known. Contact with him was immediate, intimate and rich. When he was gay, and he was often gay—my dominant memory of him is of a blithe and joyful man—he seemed to spread a sensuous enchantment about him. By a natural magic he unsealed the eyes of those in his company; birds and beasts and flowers became new-minted as in Paradise; they stood revealed as what they were, and not the poor objects of our dull and common seeing. The most ordinary domestic act—the roasting of a joint of meat, the washing up of crockery, the painting of a cottage room—in his doing became a gay sacrament.

This is the poet; and this was Lawrence.

This article is just in its estimation of his wonder: and so too was an obituary in the *Manchester Guardian*. But, considering the sowing, this is a meagre harvest that his genius reaps from contemporary fame; and it might be supposed that the *Frankfurter Zeitung* was right in the leader it published the other day, which claimed with a sneer that Lawrence was better appreciated in Germany than in England. Yet it is not so. The grief caused by his death proves far otherwise. I do not speak of his friends and his intimates. They had all cause to regret him for purely selfish reasons. Such a gay companion as the article in the *Times* Literary Supplement delineates is not easily replaced; nor such a friend.

He was completely generous. At a moment when there were not ten pounds between him and destitution he thrust five of them upon a friend and because the friend refused them, flew into a transport of high-pitched rage.

It was not only with his money he was generous. He had *caritas*. That which was needed had to be given. These traits in him would explain the grief of his friends; but another explanation, which can only lie in his genius, must be found for the effect of his death on those who had never set eyes on him. I know nobody of middle age or less, above a certain standard of intellectual integrity or imaginative vigour, who is not stricken by his loss. The prevalent feeling was well described by a young man, a critic and a poet, who said to me the other day, "I've felt rather ill ever since Lawrence died." There is the general malaise one feels after a severe shock, after a loss that cannot be made good.

How deep the experience goes can be measured by the attempts the mind made to refuse it; for everybody I know, and myself also, refused to believe the news when it came. The first threat of trouble came to me between the acts of *This Way to Paradise*, a dramatization of Aldous Huxley's

Point Counter Point. It is not so good as a play as it was as a novel. Curiously enough, although one usually thinks at a non-Shavian play that its intellectual content is pitiably below that of most novels, the dialectic stuff of this novel, which was far above the level of current fiction, seemed poor and unsatisfying when one heard it recited over the footlights. This was perhaps because Aldous Huxley's novels are, for all their simulation of realism, halfway to poetry. The characters, and the rhythm of their appearance, give an account of the phenomena in their creator's spiritual universe. Young Quarles, the intellectual who cannot satisfy his wife Elinor's need for emotion, so that she turns to Webley, the brainless man of action, represents the fantasy that vexes man with a nightmare vision in which his environment assumes a thousand forms to take his potency away from him. If he thinks, surely the power is draining away from him in a thin flood; if he turns to action, he does but bleed from a different vein; and there are always women. Old Quarles, .with his perturbed tootings, "A babah? Surely not a babah?" was the picture of the father the son makes in rebellion, the symbol of humanity that the individual invents when he desires to make the gesture of power that is his alone. These, and all the other figures of *Point Counter Point*, were real events in Aldous Huxley's mind, and the sequence in which they appeared and reappeared revealed how his argument with himself about its values was going. It was therefore acceptable by all readers who had reached a certain level of self-consciousness, by reason of the comparison and contrasts they could find between his universe and theirs.

But when these same characters and events were presented in the terribly material medium of the stage, without any disguise of poetry, one had to judge them as if they were taking place on the plane of everyday life. Then one watched the young Quarles household only to imagine how Elinor would react to the torture, hardly to be described in the humanitarian pages of an Occidental publication, though the *Chinese Police Gazette* might like it, which one has long devised for all wives who interrupt their husbands when they are working to ask them if they remember those summer evenings in the garden at Wherever eight years ago. Old Quarles was exactly as significant in comparison with all the other senile libertines the stage has seen as his lines enable him to be, and no more. The dialectic speeches, put into the mouths of those who had diminished from real poetic creations to stage types, seemed irrelevant and papery. But certain things still emerged as important. Profound meaning rang out through lines that bore relation to matters not transplanted from the novel into the play, like bells heard across a lake from a church hidden in the hills on the other side. One was con-

scious of this whenever Mark Rampion, in whom
Aldous Huxley has very obviously depicted Lawrence, came on the stage. One thought, "Even
Aldous Huxley, who is so far above the rest of us,
feels that he has to look up to Lawrence." When the
curtain fell I said as much to my companion, who
answered, "You know Lawrence is dangerously
ill." For no reason at all I replied, "Oh, I don't
believe that, it's quite impossible," just as lots of
people, equally without reason, felt confidently,
"There's some mistake," when they read in the
newspapers about his death at Vence. What would
Aldous Huxley or anybody who had seen *This Way
to Paradise* have done if they had suddenly heard
that the producers of the play had decided to cut
out the character of Mark Rampion? All alike
would have cried out that the best thing would then
be gone, that the producers could not meditate such
a folly. Even so did those of us who heard of Lawrence's death feel that from the spectacle of the
universe, by the incredible stupidity of a destroying
angel, the best thing had gone. Since we see nothing
in the universe outside us which we cannot identify
with what we see in the universe within us, this
means that the forces which moved Lawrence seem
to us the best part of our human equipment.

What were these forces? I can find an answer
most easily, I find, by referring not to his work, but
to my personal acquaintanceship with him, though

that was slight. One spring day about ten years ago I was lunching in Florence with Reggie Turner and Norman Douglas. Reggie Turner has been described by Max Beerbohm as Artemus in his paper on wits in *And Even Now*, and there is no need to add a line save to commemorate a supremely imaginative act of charity. When Oscar Wilde came out of prison, Reggie Turner sent him one of the most expensive and completely useless fitted dressing cases that Bond Street has ever achieved. There is need to tell over again the tale of Norman Douglas's accomplishments, because the mind finds them so incredible that it has a disposition to forget them. Besides being a master of English prose, he is one of the finest classical scholars in Europe, a great linguist (he can even speak and write Russian), a pianist, a composer, a caricaturist, a botanist, and a landscape gardener—all to the highest degree of accomplishment. By one of those ironies which forbids us to believe that nature is neutral, even when one has been forced to give up one's faith that she is kindly, Reggie Turner, in whose heart is innocence, wears the winking face of a devil off a quattrocento choir stall; and Norman Douglas, whose heart, so far as innocence is concerned, is as the Gobi Desert, looks as one who has never seen Dr. Cadman would imagine him to look. There are what one has been led to believe are the stigmata of moral earnestness: the penetrating eyes under level brows, compressed lips, head set sturdily between the shoulders, as if here reason were firmly rooted in the moral law, and hair white as if the scalp itself had renounced all such vanity as colour. And indeed there is here some of the quality suggested. There is in him an austere loyalty to an interpretation of life that might, if need pushed him to it, not baulk at renunciation. Less than paganism is his religion. Things are what they are. If the landscape seems to form a pattern and the figure of a god to emerge, then that does but prove that a god is but a landscape seeming to form a pattern. That being so, all things are equal and unrelated, perpetually dissolvent back to their point of least significance. Believing this he will not forswear his belief. That day at lunch his conversation perpetually made and unmade the world till late in the afternoon; and then, though there would have seemed to an observer no reason why we should ever move, we were entertaining each other so well, we rose to our feet. Lawrence was coming in by some slow train that crawled up from Rome laden with poor folks that could not pay for speed, and would by now be installed in his hotel. To each of us, different though we were in type, it appeared of paramount importance that we should go and pay him our respects at the first possible moment.

He was staying in a poorish hotel overlooking

what seems to me, since I am one of those who are
so enamoured of Rome that they will not submit
themselves to the magic of Florence, to be a trench
of drab and turbid water wholly undeserving of the
romantic prestige we have given the Arno. Make
no mistake, it was the hotel that overlooked the
Arno, not Lawrence. His room was one of the
cheaper ones at the back. His sense of guilt which
scourged him perpetually, which was the motive
power of his genius, since it made him inquire
what sin it was which he and all mankind have on
their conscience, forbade him either enjoying comfort or having the money to pay for it, lest he
should weaken. So it was a small, mean room in
which he sat tapping away at a typewriter. Norman
Douglas burst out in a great laugh as we went in
and asked him if he were already writing an article
about the present state of Florence; and Lawrence
answered seriously that he was. This was faintly
embarrassing, because on the doorstep Douglas
had described how on arriving in a town Lawrence
used to go straight from the railway station to his
hotel and immediately sit down and hammer out
articles about the place, vehemently and exhaus-
tively describing the temperament of the people.
This seemed obviously a silly thing to do, and here
he was doing it. Douglas's laughter rang out louder
than ever, and malicious as a satyr's.

But we forgot all that when Lawrence set his work aside and laid himself out to be a good host to us. He was one of the most polite people I have ever met, in both naïve and subtle ways. The other two knew him well, but I had never seen him before. He made friends as a child might do, by shyly handing me funny little boxes he had brought from some strange place he had recently visited; and he made friends too as if he were a wise old philosopher at the end of his days, by taking notice of one's personality, showing that he recognized its quality and giving it his blessing. Also there was a promise that a shy wild thing might well give and exact from its fellows, that he would live if one would let him live. Presently he settled down to give, in a curious hollow voice, like the soft hoot of an owl, an account of the journey he had made, up from Sicily to Capri, from Capri to Rome, from Rome to Florence. There seemed no reason why he should have made these journeys, which were all as uncomfortable as cheap travelling is in Italy; nor did there seem any reason why he was presently going to Baden-Baden. Yet, if every word he said disclosed less and less reason for this journeying, it also disclosed a very definite purpose. These were the journeys that the mystics of a certain type have always found necessary. The Russian saint goes to the head of his family and says good-bye and takes his stick and walks out with no objective but the truth. The Indian fakir draws lines with his bare feet across the dust of his peninsula which describe a diagram, meaningless to the uninitiated, but significant of holiness. Lawrence travelled, it seemed, to get a certain Apocalyptic vision of mankind that he registered again and again and again, always rising to a pitch of ecstatic agony. Norman Douglas, Reggie Turner, and I, none of whom would have moved from one place to another except in the greatest comfort procurable and with a definite purpose, or have endured a disagreeable experience twice if we could possibly help it, sat in a row on the bed and nodded. We knew that what he was doing was right. We nodded and were entranced.

The next day Norman Douglas and I went a walk with Lawrence far out into the country, past the Certosa. It was a joy for me to leave the city, for I cannot abide trams and Florence is congested with them. Impossible to pass through the streets without feeling that one is being dogged by a moaning tram one had betrayed in one's reckless youth; and it had been raining so hard that there had for long been no opportunity to walk in the country. Now there had been a day's sunshine, and the whole world was new. Irises thrust out of the wet earth like weapons suddenly brought into action. The cypresses, instead of being lank funereal plumes commemorating a foundered landscape, were exclamation marks drawn in Chinese ink, crying out at the beauty of the reborn countryside. About the grassy borders of the road there was much fine enamelwork in little flowers and weeds as one has seen it on the swards of Botticelli. Of the renascent quality of the day Lawrence became an embodiment. He was made in the angelic colours. His skin, though he had lived so much in the Southern countries, was very white, his eyes were light, his hair and beard were a pale luminous red. His body was very thin, and because of the flimsiness of his build it seemed as if a groove ran down the centre of his chest and his spine, so that his shoulder blades stood out in a pair of almost wing-like projections. He moved quickly and joyously. One could imagine him as a forerunner, speeding faster than spring can go from bud to bud on the bushes, to tell the world of the season that was coming to save it from winter. Beside him Norman Douglas lumbered along stockily. Because he knew what emperor had built this road and set that city on a hill, and how the Etruscans had been like minded in their buildings before him, he made one feel that there have been so many springs that in effect there is no spring, but that that is of no great moment. Bending over a filemot-coloured flower that he had not seen since he found it on Mount Olympus, his face grew nearly as tender as a mother bending over her child. When a child tumbled at his feet from the terrace of an olive orchard, his face became neither more nor less tender than before.

They moved in unison of pace along the road, these two, and chatted. They were on good terms then, Ormuzd and Ahriman.

We stopped for lunch at a place that was called the Bridge of Something: an inn that looked across a green meadow to a whitish river. We ate at a table on which a trellis of wisteria painted a shadow far more substantial than the blue mist that was its substance. The two men talked for long of a poor waif, a bastard sprig of royalty, that had recently killed himself after a life divided between conflicting passions for monastic life, unlawful pleasures, and financial fraud. He had sought refuge at the monastery of Monte Cassino, that nursery of European culture, where St. Thomas Aquinas himself was educated; but soon was obliged to flee down one side of the sugar loaf mountain while the carabinieri climbed up the other with a warrant for his arrest on charges connected with the Italian law of credit. Then he had gone to Malta, and played more fantasias on the theme of debt, till his invention was exhausted. This was the man whose recollections of service in the French Foreign Legion were published with a preface by Lawrence which provoked Norman Douglas to a savage retort that stands high among the dog fights of literary men. But then they were joined in amity while they talked of him with that grave and brotherly pitifulness that men who have found it difficult to accommodate themselves to their fellow men feel for those who have found it impossible. They broke off, I remember, to look at some lads who made their way across the meadow and began to strip by the river bank. "The water will be icy," said Douglas, "it won't be warm till the snow goes off the mountains." He began to chuckle at the thought of the shock that was coming to the boys who had been tempted by the first hot day. Lawrence let his breath hiss out through his teeth at the thought of their agony; but he seemed to find pleasure in it, as he would in any intense feeling.

Presently we rose and went on our way. Norman Douglas took the landlord's hand and wrung it heartily, saying a fervid good-bye. Lawrence exclaimed, "Douglas, how can you shake hands with these people!" He meant by this that the antipathy between the Northern and the Southern peoples was so great that there could be no sincere attempt at friendship with them. Douglas answered with a grin, "Oh, it takes something off the bill next time." He did not mean that. It was simply the first way that came to hand of saying that he would not get excited about these fine points, that in his universe every phenomenon was of equal value. We walked away. After a minute or two I looked back through the olive trees and saw the landlord standing where we had left him, sending after us a hard black Italian stare. "Do you know, Douglas," said Lawrence suddenly, though he had not looked back, "I

can't help thinking that the man understood English." "Oh, no," I said falsely, "I'm sure he didn't."
But Douglas, laughing more deeply than ever, said,
"I got that too." We all walked along without speaking, ill at ease, though Douglas kept his eyes crinkled
as if he were still laughing. Ormuzd and Ahriman
alike did not want unnecessary explosions of the
forces they well knew to be latent in their universe.

Later Lawrence began to talk of the Sicilian peasants and how full of hatred and malice he had found
them. There was a great tale about some old crones
who had come up at twilight to his house in Taor-
mina with some jars of honey they had wanted him
to buy, and had crouched down on his terrace while
he tested their goods with malignity in their eyes, in
their squatting bodies. They had meant to cheat
him, for it was last year's honey and ill preserved.
He detected the fraud in an instant, with his sturdy
wisdom about household matters, and bade them
be gone. Silently they rose and filed out through his
olive trees with their jars on their shoulders, with
increased malignity in their eyes and in their
prowling bodies, because they had not been able to
cheat him. "Such hatred!" he cried in effect.
"Such black loathing." Again I felt embarrassed,
as I did when we discovered him pounding out
articles on the momentary state of Florence with
nothing more to go on than a glimpse at it. Surely
he was now being almost too flatly silly, even a little

mad? Of course peasants try to cheat one over honey
or anything else, in Italy or anywhere else, and very
natural it is, considering how meagrely the earth
gives up its fruits. But as for hatred and black loathing, surely this is persecution mania? I was a little
unhappy about it, which was a pity, for that made
an unsatisfactory ending to what was to be my
last meeting with Lawrence, though mercifully
not my last contact with him. For a few months ago
I received a letter from him thanking me for some
little tribute I had paid him during the trouble
about his pictures in London. This letter showed the
utmost humility in him to take notice of such a small
courtesy; and it showed more than that. With
marvellous sensitiveness he had deduced from a
phrase or two in my article that I was troubled by a
certain problem, and he said words that in their
affectionate encouragement and exquisite appositeness could not have been bettered if we had spent
the ten years that had intervened since our meeting
in the closest friendship.

The point about Lawrence's work that I have
been unable to explain save by resorting to my
personal acquaintance with him is this: that it was
founded on the same basis as those of his mental
movements which then seemed to me ridiculous,
and which, now that I have had more experience,
I see as proceeding in a straight line to the distant
goal of wisdom. He was tapping out an article on

the state of Florence at that moment without knowing enough about it to make his views of real value.
Is that the way I looked at it? Then I was naïve.
I know now that he was writing about the state of
his own soul at that moment, which, since our self-
consciousness is incomplete, and since in consequence our vocabulary also is incomplete, he could
only render in symbolic terms; and the city of
Florence was as good a symbol as any other. If he
was foolish in taking the material universe and making allegations about it that were true only of the
universe within his own soul, then Rimbaud was a
great fool also. Or to go further back, so too was
Dante, who made a new Heaven and Hell and
Purgatory as a symbol for the geography within
his own breast, and so too was St. Augustine, when
in *The City of God* he writes an attack on the pagan
world, which is unjust so long as it is regarded as an
account of events on the material plane, but which
is beyond price as an account of the conflict in his
soul between that which tended to death and that
which tended to life. Lawrence was in fact no different from any other great artist who has felt the
urgency to describe the unseen so keenly that he has
rifled the seen of its vocabulary and diverted it to
that purpose; and it took courage to do that in a
land swamped with naturalism as England was when
Lawrence began to write.

When he cried out at Douglas for shaking hands

with the innkeeper because the North and the South were enemies, and when he saw the old crones who had come to cheat him out of an odd lira or two over the honey as mænads too venomous even to be flamboyant, I thought he was seeing lurid colours that were in his eye and not in the universe he looked on. Now I think he was doing justice to the seriousness of life, and had been rewarded with a deeper insight into its nature than most of us have. If one has the dislike of any proof that the universe has structure which is the mark of an incoherent mind, then one will find something very distasteful in his assumption that John Smith and Giovanni Grimaldi are not merely individuals, but are parts of two systems of life so fundamentally opposed that their minutest constituents must also be in opposition. If one has no purpose and therefore does not need to know the relationship between the forces of the mind and events in the external world, then it is as well to say that the old women out for liras were simply old women out for liras, and leave it at that. But if one hopes that some day the mind shall govern life, then it is of value that one shall be shown a small instance of the sadism that makes the human being rejoice in killing, hurting, robbing its neighbour, and that one shall be told that this is as horrible as war, since war also is the fruit of this sadism; and that therefore the mind must walk proudly and always armed, that it shall not be robbed of its power. There is nothing disconcerting about these or any other of Lawrence's attitudes, if one is a true inheritor of tradition and realizes that the greatest sons of man have always recognized that the mind which is his house is ablaze and that if the fire is not put out he will perish. Then one will rejoice that our age produced one artist who had the earnestness of the patristic writers, who like them could know no peace till he had discovered what made men lust after death. He laboured under a disadvantage compared with the fathers, in his lack of a vocabulary of symbolic terms such as was given them by theology; in the allegory of the death of the soul which ends with the death of Gerald among the mountains in *Women in Love*, he cannot tell his story save by the clumsy creation of images that do not give up their meaning till the book has been read many times. But even these struggles are of value, since they recall to one the symbolic nature of all thought. Knowledge is but a translation of reality into terms comprehensible by the human mind, a grappling with a mystery. None undertake it with the courage of Lawrence unless they very greatly care.

His claim to our reverence and gratitude was not in the least part diminished by *Lady Chatterly's Lover*. It is an appalling fact that man should speak of the functions on which depend the continued existence of his species and the tender life of the heart in words that cause shame and ugly laughter when they are spoken. When Lawrence's pity was aroused by this wound in the side of life he did what saints do: he asked for a miracle. He laid sex and those base words for it on the salver of his art and held them up before the consciousness of the world, which was his way of approaching creation, and prayed that both might be transmuted to the highest that man could use. There are many people like myself who feel that his prayer was in vain: that those words were nothing but the expressions of hatred felt by the will to die for the will to live, and they could never be converted to anything else. But people like myself are infinitely lesser than Lawrence. The presumption is that if he did not reach the truth he at least came nearer it than we did. In any case, it was the special merit of this and all his other works, as I can see by looking back at our meeting and measuring the change in my attitude towards his characteristic traits, that in no way did he underrate the gravity of the human situation.

As I write there comes to me this week's issue of *Time and Tide*, and I find in it a letter about Lawrence, from Catherine Carswell, an infrequent but gifted writer—her note on Duse in the *Adelphi* was one of the finest pieces of dramatic criticism I have ever read. Her letter is worth reprinting.

Sir:

*The picture of D. H. Lawrence suggested by the obituary notices
of "competent critics" is of a man morose, frustrated, tortured,
even a sinister failure. Perhaps this is because any other view would
make his critics look rather silly. Anyhow, to those who knew him,
and I knew him since 1914 as friend, hostess and guest in varying
circumstances, often of the most trying kind, at home and abroad,
that picture would be comic if it were not in the circumstances
disgraceful.*

*Lawrence was as little morose as an open clematis flower, as
little tortured or sinister or hysterical as a humming bird. Gay,
skilful, clever at everything, furious when he felt like it but never
grieved or upset, intensely amusing, without sentimentality or affectation, almost always right in his touch for the* content *of things
or persons, he was at once the most harmonious and the most
vital person I ever saw.*

*As to frustration, consider his achievements. In the face of
formidable initial disadvantages and lifelong delicacy, poverty
that lasted for three quarters of his life and hostility that survives
his death, he did nothing that he did not really want to do, and
all that he most wanted to do he did. He went all over the world,
he owned a ranch, he lived in the most beautiful corners of Europe,
and met whom he wanted to meet and told them that they were
wrong and that he was right. He painted and made things and
sang and rode. He wrote something like three dozen books, of
which even the worst pages dance with life that could be mistaken
for no other man's, while the best are admitted, even by those who
hate him, to be unsurpassed. Without vices, with most human
virtues, the husband of one wife, scrupulously honest, this estimable
citizen yet managed to keep free from the shackles of civilization
and the cant of literary cliques. He would have laughed lightly and
cursed venomously in passing at the solemn owls—each one
secretly chained by the leg—who now conduct his inquest. To do*

his work and lead his life in spite of them took some doing, but he did it, and long after they are forgotten, sensitive and innocent people—if any are left—will turn Lawrence's pages and know from them what sort of a rare man Lawrence was.

CATHERINE CARSWELL.

We must ourselves be grievously defeated if we do not regard the life of D. H. Lawrence as a spiritual victory.

W HEN I read in Professor Elmer More's article on "A Revival of Humanism" in the March *Bookman*, the phrase "the ignorant and conceited outburst of Mr. Allen Tate," I said to myself, "I think I shall have to go." When I read in the "Chronicle and Comment" of the same number the ironic comment, "which is to say that T. S. Eliot, Paul E. More, and Jacques Maritain, for instance, are less intelligent than Edmund Wilson, which is absurd," I said, "I shall have to go." When I read further on in the same article a phrase referring to the writers who have been rebutting the humanist attack in other papers: "After all, their backs are against the wall, for if a few managing editors become aware of how things are going, there will be some highly talented literary critics pounding the pavement," I said, "Lo! I have gone." Spiritually I was already pounding the pavement and proud to be doing so.

I object to Professor Paul Elmer More's phrase regarding Mr. L. Allen Tate, not because I am modest enough to think I ought to hide when ignorance and conceit are denounced, but because I find the phrase incomprehensible as a description of Mr. Tate's article and unpleasantly incongruous on lips self-dedicated to restraint and decorum. I object to the tone and content of the comparison drawn between Edmund Wilson and the three other critics because their implications strike at the root of criticism. To begin with, I do not agree with the attempted disparagement of Edmund Wilson. I submit that there are no grounds for supposing that T. S. Eliot could have written anything on a par with the articles on the moderns which Edmund Wilson has recently contributed to the *New Republic*. There is no evidence that he would have been equal to such a sustained effort. To judge from his restricted field of reference he could not have covered the ground; and such authors as he dealt with would have had to fear that remarkable power of misunderstanding which has led him into certain comic misreadings of individual passages in Shelley and Swinburne, and of the entire significance of Benda and Maurras. Those who have preferred familiarity with Mr. Eliot's work to blind admiration for it know that the part of his criticism that repays attention either is slight and charming and purely impressionistic (like his *Dante*) or consists of reproductions rather than developments of the ideas of Professor More and Professor Babbitt. The rest is a flustered search for coherence disingenuously disguised by a style which suggests that he has found it. Beside this literary personality Edmund Wilson does not show to disadvantage. Indubitably Professor More is a greater scholar and philosopher than Edmund Wilson. It is, however, obvious from his references to modern French literature that he also could not have covered the ground of these particular articles; and we have reason to believe it would have been impossible for him to have judged any series of modern phenomena with the detachment shown by Edmund Wilson. It is to be feared that emotion would have led him to reactions as uncontrolled by reason as his use of the phrase "pseudo-scientific treatises," in referring to the work of Mr. I. A. Richards, a scholar of academic distinction fully equal to that of Professor More at the same age. In the comparison to M. Maritain we reap the consequences of one of Mr. Eliot's misrepresentations of French writers. It is untrue that M. Maritain enjoys anything like the pre-eminence as a philosopher in France that Mr. Eliot has informed his generation. There are higher and purer sources of Aquinism. As those of us know who have attended M. Maritain's lectures, he is charming and persuasive beyond belief but he has only the virtues of the popular preacher, and he is not with-

out the defects of the type. It is unfortunately impossible to conceive him writing anything so little
determined by its effect on the sensibilities of the
reader as Mr. Wilson's articles.

Even more objectionable than this underrating of
a writer who possesses in such high degrees the
qualities that justify writing—a will to find the truth
and a brain that is an efficient instrument for the
search—I find the incident that provokes the judgment. What has brought down contempt on Edmund Wilson's head is his opinion that it is no longer
possible for a first-rate mind to accept the supernatural basis of religion. In other words, the writer
of "Chronicle and Comment" refuses to respect the
spiritual struggles which have led Edmund Wilson
to arrive at the conclusion that it is not possible for a
first-rate mind to accept the supernatural basis of
religion, yet he is willing to respect the spiritual
struggles which have led T. S. Eliot to the conclusion that it is. But surely the progress of art and
science depends on our respecting spiritual struggles
only in so far as the protagonist shows by his
dialectical conduct that he will accept all truth that
he discovers in the course of his struggle, regardless
of the extent to which it tallies with his previous
prepossessions. Certainly Edmund Wilson, in his
patient research into original sources and his loyalty
to logic, to name but two of his qualities, shows a
high standard of dialectical conduct. The deprecia-

tion of him compared with three persons whose superiority in these matters is so disputable suggests that we have strayed into a world, not high in the intellectual cosmogony, where it is held that certain beliefs are in themselves a certificate of mental gentility. Those who hold them are entitled to look at persons of equal gifts and attainments who do not hold them as, in another world (hardly, it seems to me, less respectable), persons who are on the Social Register look at persons not on the Social Register. In this intellectual world it is regrettably the case that bigoted Protestants despise persons who ought not to be despised, such as Valéry and Claudel, because they are Roman Catholics; and bigoted Roman Catholics despise most of English and American literature because it is written by Protestants; and the editor of the *Bookman* writes in "Chronicle and Comment" concerning his opponents: "After all, their backs are against the wall, for if a few managing editors become aware of how things are going, there will be some highly talented literary critics pounding the pavement."

I am not aware of the full list of opponents, but I know it includes Edmund Wilson, T. S. Matthews, Henry Hazlitt, Babette Deutsch, Burton Rascoe, John Chamberlain, Malcolm Cowley, and Carl van Doren. Most of these writers are personally unknown or very slightly known to me. Some of them are hostile to me. But I know their work and its level of intellectual integrity; and it seems to me that ascription of such motives to them is poor dialectical conduct. Again I would complain of the incongruity of such phrases on lips self-dedicated to decorum and restraint.

But even if these expressions had not seemed to me extremely unlike those which should be employed to create an atmosphere proper for the discussion of art and science, I fear that I should be uneasy in a periodical devoted to the propagation of humanism. This is not because I am hostile to its ostensible end: the maintenance of tradition. I would point as a certificate of my soundness in this respect to the fact that in my own country my implacable foes are Mr. Arnold Bennett and Mr. St. John Ervine and Mr. Edward Garnett. I do not, however, find that humanism is likely to maintain tradition as satisfactorily as the modern writers— Proust, Joyce, Lawrence, Virginia Woolf, Aldous Huxley, to name but a few—whom it so sweepingly repudiates.

It seems to me—and here it takes some courage to put down my findings, in view of the controversially archaic disposition of humanists to answer the mildest criticism with accusations of "impudence"— that humanism is too much in the nature of an apostolic following of two men, both of whom are singularly unfitted, owing to eccentricities of their dialectical conduct, to act as guide to tradition through this age. I am well aware that Professor Irving Babbitt and Professor Paul Elmer More are among the most learned men now living. This learning does not, however, prevent them from labouring under certain disqualifications which forbid them to understand contemporary life and letters. Professor Irving Babbitt gave me a shock in that respect which I have never forgotten, when I read *Rousseau and Romanticism*. That book builds up out of the immense resources of scholarship a case against the movement for the sanctification of ecstasy and the discrediting of intellect which Rousseau initiated and transmitted to the nineteenth century. I enjoyed it thoroughly. But what I could not understand was the tone of superiority and querulousness with which the case was conducted. Throughout the book Professor Babbitt's manner was that of one who disdainfully outlines a point of view peculiar to a small group of the saved and anathema to the general. Yet I cannot think of anybody literate, except Mr. Middleton Murry and his followers, who holds a contrary opinion.

Looking back to my schooldays, I remembered that my literature master had never ceased to try to influence our taste against the emotional excesses of the romantic movement. We were always warned that while we might find Keats and Shelley and Byron satisfying in our youth, later on we would see the superiority of a steady lamp to fireworks. "If you cannot read Milton when you are older," said Mr. Budge in good Scots idiom, "never let on you were pupils of mine." The uncontrolled exuberance of Bulwer Lytton and Disraeli, ot George Sand and Lamartine and Musset, afforded opportunity for a great many quite good jokes, which were coupled with fair-minded recognition of those writers' fine qualities. Thackeray's guy of Goethe's *Werther* ("Charlotte like a perfect lady Went on cutting bread and butter") was recited with acclamation. This attitude towards Romanticism was not peculiar to this master. Over the way, in the history classroom, I remember, the master told us of Victor Hugo's comic proceedings during the Coup d'Etat and clearly gave us to understand that he owed his ridiculousness to participation in a ridiculous movement. At the time I read *Rousseau and Romanticism* and was startled by its affectation of eclecticism I questioned my two sisters who had been educated some years earlier than myself, not in Scotland but in England, one at a high school and one at a famous boarding school, and found that they had been indoctrinated with the very same sensible opinions. Professor W. P. Ker once said to me in a conversation on this topic: "It has been the standard attitude during my lifetime." So thoroughly did we have this point of view drummed into

us that nearly all of us found it difficult to read Rousseau because of his emotional fanfaronades, and
had to be seduced into doing so by the good Marley.
None of us, I think, did so without having received
innumerable warnings from our youth up that
what he said concerning the angelic nature of the
natural man was dubious. In other words, the point
of view that Professor Babbitt peevishly exhibits as
a rare jewel which the world is not fit to own is
about as rare as a nickel.

Another example of a similar baseless claim is
contained in Professor Babbitt's *Democracy and
Leadership*. I challenge anyone to examine the files
of the English Tory paper, the *Morning Post*, for
the last thirty years and be able to detect any difference between the philosophy which inspired the
persons responsible for its leaders and its policy and
Professor Babbitt's philosophy as expressed in that
book. Both take their stand on what Professor Babbitt identifies as the distinction between humanism
and humanitarianism and the condemnation of the
latter. That was the position on which the late Lord
Milner and the late Professor A. V. Dicey (to select
but two names out of hundreds that offer) based a
series of attacks on the *Zeitgeist* very much in Professor Babbitt's vein. It was the position on which
the late Lord Balfour took his stand, but, since he
was an abler and more experienced statesman than

any of these three, found an inspiration for coöperation not attack on the *Zeitgeist;* and to that we owe
his lifelong attempts to coördinate the ideals of
aristocracy and democracy by urging aristocrats to
submit themselves to the discipline of control to
which demos has long submitted, and by urging
democrats to submit themselves to the preparation
to which aristocracy has long submitted. It is a
position of which the newest generation is not ignorant. It is laid before school children in their civics
classes; it is laid before every adolescent likely to
play a part in politics in debates at the Oxford and
Cambridge Unions, at the London School of
Economics, the Workers' Educational Association,
Independent Labour Party local meetings—there is
no end to the occasions. If Professor Babbitt were to
appear before them and tell them that they must
have standards, and that they must get these standards "by coöperation of intellect and imagination"
and by disciplining the "feelings or affections, to use
the older words, to some ethical centre," they would
very heartily agree and explain that they were very
diligently seeking for the best means of ensuring
that coöperation and locating that ethical centre.
He would, if he pressed the matter further, find that
they were no more enthusiastic Rousseauists than
himself; and that one of the chief reasons that the
Liberal party had died was that they were just as
sceptical as he was of humanitarianism. If he

imagined that that faith has much to do with the contemporary Labour party, he would have a rude disillusionment. Again, the precious pearl of wisdom which we are shown as an act of condescension turns out to be a truism which is not often stated only because it is so generally accepted.

Professor Babbitt in his attitude to his contemporaries closely resembles the luckless soldier one has sometimes seen on a parade ground, who fails to hear the last order and goes on performing the last order but one, convinced that everybody in the regiment is out of step except himself. It is unusual to make such a soldier a drill sergeant. It is true that acceptance of Professor Babbitt's main thesis will do nobody any harm. To prefer Aristotle to Rousseau is certainly the way of grace, and though most of us would do that in any case it illumines argument to have Professor Babbitt state the case again with his unrivalled power of allusion: and similarly we can enjoy reiteration on these terms of the truism that it is better to be sane than mad. ("To lack sanity," he somewhere helpfully explains, "is to be headed towards misery and even madness.") But to accept his attitude towards the moderns seems to me a pity. It consists mainly, of course, of disapproving generalizations, but when he touches the concrete he often surprises us by his naïveté. He ranges wide, and his taste is far from being an infallible guide. Here is an instance where

he strays into consideration of another art than
literature:

The partisans of expression as opposed to form in the
eighteenth century led to the fanatics of expression in the
nineteenth century, and these have led to the maniacs of
expression in the twentieth. The extremists in painting
have gone so far beyond Cézanne, who was regarded not
so long ago as one of the wildest of innovators, that
Cézanne is, we are told, "in a fair way to achieve the
unhappy fate of becoming a classic."

Just how genuinely sensitive to art Professor Babbitt
is can be judged from this unfortunate reference to
the heir of Poussin, who was despised only because
he conflicted with the romantic movement against
which, in theory, Professor Babbitt has such an
immediate and fastidious reaction. No, I have no
great confidence in this drill sergeant.

As for the other leader of humanism, I approach
him with even greater respect and misgiving. Every
lettered person must feel the deepest gratitude to the
author of *The Greek Tradition*, not only for its mas-
terly coördination of religion and philosophy and its
easy collation of fascinating historical material, but
for its power to communicate what had seemed
nearly incommunicable, in language limpid as
spring water. Only the other day I heard a discussion that might have lingered on for weeks and then
have ended inconclusively, crisply resolved and sent

on to another stage by citation of a footnote from
Christ the Word.

I must say [he appends to his statement that the
Christian religion began with a myth] that by the use of
the word "myth" nothing is implied prejudicial to the
truth of the event designated. It simply means that any
commingling of the two spheres of the divine and the
human, any revelation of God to man, must assume an
anthropomorphic character.

I noted that all parties concerned delayed for a
moment to admire the grasp of intellectual process
that lay behind those two sentences, and that those
who knew the volumes had to say what pleasure they
had derived from them. Paul Elmer More the
Platonist is a centre of light, whom one can neglect
only at a heavy cost to oneself. I am sure of that.
But I am equally sure that Paul Elmer More the
critic of modern literature is a guide that one can
follow only at heavy cost to oneself.

One cannot read for long in *Shelburne Essays*
without coming on phrases that are highly embarrassing to one's reverence for Professor More.
Sooner or later one comes on phrases as odd as this:
"Longfellow, we are told by his biographer, wrote
but a single love poem (and I, for one, am ready to
honour him for this reserve) . . ." Why, one wonders, should Professor More respect a poet for
"reserve" because he writes only one of a sort of

poem not necessarily associated with lack of that
quality?—particularly when that one essay, as Professor More points out, shows that quality to excess.
One wonders still more when one reads in his essay
on "The Irish Movement": "There is one trick of
both (though it is much more marked in Mr.
Yeats)" (Professor More had coupled the names of
Mr. Yeats and Arthur Symons on the basis of a resemblance between them which was, no doubt, more
apparent then than it is now) "which may seem
trivial, and yet does in some way connect itself with
the total impression of their art. This is an insistence
on the hair in describing women. Just why this
habit should smack of decadence is not quite clear
to me, but the feeling it inspires is unmistakable.
Out of curiosity I counted the number of allusions
to hair in the few poems that make up Mr. Yeats's
Wind Among the Reeds and found they mounted up to
twenty-three." There follow phrases that are some of
them otiose and some of them commonplace, but
that none of them could evoke in any rational mind
the description "troubling and unwholesome" applied to them by Professor More.

To dwell on these oddities is not to number oneself among cavillers who see nothing of the sun but
the spots on it. For they are not superficial. They
are the minor effects of a tendency in Professor More
which has major effects in plenty. It is a tendency to
raise a fog of feeling in front of certain aspects of

humanity instead of facing them calmly and exercising the faculty of judgment in the clear light of reason. Sometimes this leads to blindness regarding æsthetic matters he is committed to discuss. For example, he becomes so excited over Arthur Symons's lachrymose pretensions to promiscuity that he quotes one of his most dreadful poems ("White girl, your flesh is lilies Under a frozen moon, So still is The rapture of your swoon Of whiteness, snow or lilies," and so, very regrettably, on) without any of the called for comminations. I am not, be it understood, complaining that Professor More is prudish. There is something very far from prudery in the good sense and good breeding with which he refuses to accept Austin Dobson's ululations against poor Hazlitt's *Liber Amoris*. In point of fact, there are more allusions to sex in *Shelburne Essays* than one will find in, let us say, the critical works of Mr. I. A. Richards. This is of no particular significance, one way or the other, since there is no obligation in any author to write about the subject or keep silence on it. The aspects of life which Professor More refuses to face are far deeper and wider than the single element of sexual behaviour, as he states in one of the most memorable passages in modern literature:[1]

---

[1]Seward Collins, in his reply to this article, made a disingenuous attempt to prove that in this passage Professor More was describing the attitude of others and not his own. There is no support for this view in the context; and indeed he has taken full responsibility for this attitude in many other parts of his writings.

But now at last [he writes of the effect of evolutionary theory] we are shocked out of our serenity. We are made conscious of the shame of the hidden past, and the ancient haunting terror is revealed in all its hideous nakedness. Have you ever by chance strayed through a museum where the relics of old-world life are gathered together— filthy amphibians armed with impenetrable scales, grotesque serpents eight fathoms long that churned the seas, huge reptiles that beat the air with wings of nightmare breadth! The imagination recoils from picturing what the world must have been when Nature exhausted herself to fashion these abhorrent monstrosities. We have burrowed the soil and brought into the light of day these reluctant hidden records of bestial growth. Consider for a moment what it would mean if some new geology should lay bare the covered strata of memory in our own brain corresponding to these records of the earth, for there is nothing lost, and in some mysterious way the memories of all that obscure past are stored up within us. If evolution is true, we are the inheritors in our soul of the experience and life of those innumerable generations whose material forms lie moulded in the bedrock of the earth. Consider the horror of beholding in our consciousness the remembrance of such fears and frenzies, such cruel passions and wallowing desires as would correspond to these gigantic and abortive relics of antiquity. Would not the world in its shame cry out for some Lethean draught of sleep, though it were as profound as the oblivion of Nirvana? This is the terror, then, that from the beginning has beset the upholders of religion, and has caused them to attack the revelations of natural science; for what faith or beauty of holiness can abide after such an uncovering? None, unless to obtain spiritual grace the whole memory and personality of a man can be blotted out, and the spirit be severed from the experience of the body by an impassable gulf. And I think the shadow of this dread is typified in the curse which Noah laid upon his son Ham.

Is this really the expression of a mind that one could trust as guide to contemporary art—that is, to the future? I pass over the extremely curious spiritual implications of the passage, though I would give much to hear some sturdy Roman Catholic opinion on a believer who so signally failed to perform "an act of resignation to the divine will" by this wholesale rejection of creation, and who took the doctrine of original sin as a reason for evading the duty of self-examination. Nor will I dwell on the oddity of finding in an avowed anti-emotionalist a passage which is so nearly a pure shriek of emotion. It is more relevant to our discussion to note the oddity in an avowed traditionalist of this perfervid cult of the moment. For the paragraph is, of course, a confession of present-worship. Professor More says that he will have nothing to do with human nature except as it is at the moment, or as it was at such moments in the past when it took forms that are consonant with its current notions of its dignity. This programme is most nourishing to our complacence. We ourselves at our present stage of development are being taken as the centre of the universe. But unfortunately it does more than regret the past, it makes an attack on the present which is none the less mischievous for being indirect. For our present is as inextricably fused with the past by descent as a child with its mother. Parts of the present declare their relationship with the past without disguise, and in considering them we look straight down a shaft into the darkness of the primitive heart. If we abandon ourselves to Professor More's attitude we are bound to do as he does and refuse to consider them calmly and gravely, and to raise about them a fog of feeling in which the judgment cannot operate. Other parts of the present do not so visibly declare their relationship with the past; and for these, if we abandon ourselves to Professor More's attitude, we will inevitably be tempted to falsify an origin. We will also be tempted to regard philosophical beliefs and social and economic arrangements not as experimental adjustments forced on man by his inner need to adjust himself to the universe, each to be judged according to its success in helping him to realize this judgment, but as the noblest conceivable of ethical achievements, which it would be sacrilege to alter. Here again is a condition in which the judgment cannot operate; and for proof that it does not we have only to read Professor More's curiously passionate and unconvincing attack on Goldie Lowes Dickinson's mild reformism in the *Shelburne Essays*. Since our judgment is the one weapon we are given to ensure that the present shall not be a prelude to disaster, this attitude is a form of racial suicide.

But even more murderous is the effect of Professor More's attitude on the future; and one can see the blow being delivered in the requirements he makes of modern art. Works of art, we learn, must show man as possessed of free will and must subscribe to the theory of dual nature. The mind cannot imagine a single step more likely to damage mankind than that philosophy should claim the right to make art do propaganda for her. It is the business of philosophy to establish what truths she can so that the artist growing up within the sphere of her influence starts work as close to reality as possible; and it is her business to examine the truths established by his creations to see what bearing they have on those of her own finding. But the conceptions of philosophy are so much coarser than those of art that it is infinitely distressing to see them thrust on the artist. How crude, for example, are the conceptions of free will and dualism compared with the conceptions relating to character which lie behind the persons invented by Turgeniev. One wonders what reasons Professor More would give for the existence of art. If it is to repeat parrot-wise what philosophy teaches it, surely it merely makes tautological repetition of philosophical argument. Yet surely if there was one thing obvious about art it is that it is called into being because there are truths which

the mind finds too subtle, too awful, too disturbing
to grasp save under the reconciling remoteness of
symbolic representations staged by the imagination; and that it is above all novelty that lends the
truth subtlety, awfulness, and the power to disturb.
For this reason those who try to make the artist
work to a programme decided by the philosophers
and moralists do not represent knowledge guiding
ignorance, but knowingness leading wisdom round
in circles.

Indeed the *Bookman*, now that it has become a
trade journal for humanism, is no place for me.
Not only do I find the movement unsatisfactory in
its main personalities, I find it likely to exercise a
pernicious influence on the literature of the next few
years, and I wish to take none of the blame. Humanism, with its claims to a final "traditional wisdom"
which in their magnitude remind one of the Hum-
bert millions, with its contemptuous dismissal of all
contemporary writers who are trying to hand on
tradition, is going to do incalculable harm to the
sensitive and gifted young man who feels that he
can write, finds it difficult to start writing, and is
eaten up by a sense of inferiority to those who have
found performance possible. He will be encouraged
to convert this sense of inferiority to a sense of
superiority not by creation but by subscription to a
very easy faith. One will then have a world of T. S.
Eliots who have not achieved "The Waste Land,"

who are sterile and complacent. They may make
some attempts to carry out this new receipt of creating works of art to exhibit the beauty of the conception of free will, but this is such a breach of
tradition that as a traditionalist I have little faith in
the result. Most of the time will be spent in preaching
the pure doctrine. That is to say, the excellencies
of Professor Babbitt and Professor More will be
celebrated as continually as they have been in the
recent issues of the *Bookman*. Rousseauism, which
nobody but Mr. Middleton Murry believes in, will
be denounced as if everybody but Mr. Middleton
Murry believed in it, and so too will monism and
determinism, particularly in their relationship to
art, which is of negligible importance. Persons
believed, probably on the deluded testimony of Mr.
Eliot, to be in sympathy with humanism, will be as
warmly praised as fellow soldiers in a united army,
even when—like M. Benda, M. Jacques Maritain,
and M. Maurras—their interest in it is infinitesimal
and they are so hopelessly at odds over all issues that
it would be impossible to persuade them to sit
down at the same table. Persons vaguely believed to
be out of sympathy with the movement will, on the
other hand, be denounced on principle, without
scrutiny of their relationship.

I cannot smother the suspicion that in the course
of time this routine will be found a little dull. There
will be more and more wrangles as to who is firm in

the faith and who is not, such as the discussion involving Eliot and Maurras and Professor Babbitt in the "Chronicle and Comment" of the March *Bookman*. It is a weakness of the flesh, no doubt, but such wrangles are not universally found amusing or edifying. After a few years of the humanist régime the younger generation will inevitably be so bored that they will stampede humanism out of existence and rush back to the moderns. Joyce and Lawrence and Huxley and Virginia Woolf will be the gods of their worship, and we will have to go over the twenties all over again. No, they will probably go back to the teens, to Wells and Shaw and Galsworthy, and the thirties, when asked what they did in the Great War of the intellect by the editor of the *Bookman* who is ushering in the forties, will have to answer that they put back the clock; and sent up the first edition prices of *Ulysses* to the skies.

It occurs to me that the state of affairs which humanism threatens to precipitate in America resembles that which exists in certain circles to-day in France. There Maurras and Gide and Massis and Lasserre and Benda and Seillère and Maritain all proclaim themselves the classicists, in possession of the full tradition of mankind, and cry out on the romanticists who have repudiated it, exactly in the same manner as Professor Babbitt and Professor More. It is worth while looking twice at this army and seeing what credit it does to the cause. We will find that Maurras and Gide are at daggers drawn, and so too are Gide and Massis; while Lasserre is shocked (as well he ought to be) at the crude nineteenth-century rationalism of Benda, and Seillère and Maritain are at intellectual fisticuffs. Can it be that this situation is an inevitable consequence of abandonment to this apparently noble tourney, the war between classicism and romanticism? Can it be that there is something false in the proposition debated, which automatically commits both its defenders and its assailants to absurdity? There is good ground for the suspicion. All these people complain with an air of peevish superiority that the romantic "comes into being where sensibility usurps the function to which it is foreign, and not content with feeding and furnishing the soul with the warmth of life it requires, busies itself in steering it," and classicism represents the workings of a mind where sensibility is properly subordinated to the intelligence. But it is significant that the words I have quoted are to be found in an essay by Maurras, whose exuberant style (as we see in *Anthinéa* and *Chemin de Paradis*) and swashbuckling political activities prove him the reincarnation of Victor Hugo.[1]

Incongruities such as that make it timely for us

---

[1] This passage provoked an inquiry from Mr. Collins which is really too good to be lost. "Can that mild, deaf, scholarly recluse really be pictured as swashbuckling?" he asked. This of the most audacious demagogue of our century, who personally gave *les camelots du roi* their orders and supervised such

to remember that we all want to have a mind that works coolly and under control; that we are apt to pretend to ourselves that we have it; and that we are equally apt to heighten our pride in our fancied possession by pretending that other people are not so well endowed. The battle between romanticism and classicism is perhaps only a dramatization of this very elementary human tendency on a pretentious level, which in order to assume dignity and find a justification links up with an intellectual confusion. For there has surely been established, on purely terminological grounds, a false connection between the romantic movement initiated by Rousseau (which certainly did represent a danger to the human mind in the rashness and inexactitude of its dialectical conduct) and that dual process in art, the two parts of which we call romanticism and classicism. The first part of that process consists of recognition of new material by the artist. He exposes his intellect and his emotions to a new stimulus, he finds expression for his new reaction. The effort is disturbing to himself and to others. It breaks the mould of the universe as it was before this new experience was added to it. Then he is a romantic. If he remakes the mould of the universe,

roguish pleasantries as interference with the files of the Vatican! Mr. Collins might as appropriately have applied the phrase to Mussolini. There is something very odd indeed about the encyclopædic knowledge of European literature enjoyed by Mr. Eliot and his friends.

incorporating the new experience and reëstablishing the order which he had previously undone, he is a classicist. Both these phases can be found in a single work of art, if it is of the highest order. Both of them can be found in an artist's output as a whole, if he is a great artist. Sometimes an artist performs the first part of the process, and another the second. Sometimes to see it in its completeness one has to look not to individual artists, but to a movement, a school, even a civilization. It is therefore no use denouncing the romantic. He is a necessary precursor of the classic. If he has fairly analyzed the experience which is his subject and synthesized his findings into a true work of art, it is no use complaining because he has disturbed the universe. Harmony will come later. Art promises this, and it is the high joy of humanity that it has fulfilled its promise. Some years ago I committed myself to this view of romanticism and classicism in the *Herald Tribune*, and I stick by it.

When the shrieks of laughter have died down, and the first crop of sniggers at the "ladies" and the exquisite humours of their attempts at criticism have been got over, I will explain why I stick to it with extreme obstinacy. I stick to it because I find it is held by Paul Valery also. It has been stated by him in an introduction to *Les Fleurs du Mal* which has been republished in *Variété II:*

There is an infinity of ways by which one can define, or think one defines, the classicist. We adopt to-day this definition: *the classicist is the writer who carries a critic within himself, and who associates him ultimately with his labours.* There was a Boileau in Racine or an image of Boileau.

What is this, after all, except *to exercise selection* on romanticism, and to discern in it a good and a bad, a false and a true, failings and virtues, to do in respect of the authors of the first part of the nineteenth century what men in the time of Louis XIV have done in respect of the authors of the sixteenth century. *All classicism assumes an anterior romanticism.* All the advantages that are attributed to it, all the objections that one makes to "classical" art, are relative to this axiom: *The essence of classicism is to come after.*

And so on, here and elsewhere. I accept his authority because he is a great poet, a creator. That gives him an authority that the orthodox pro-classic participants in the discussion are without. For of Maurras, Gide, Massis, Lasserre, Benda, Seillère, and Maritain, only Gide is a creator; and he is so distraught a seeker after novelty in his creations that he gives no reassurance. It is true that Jean Moréas was associated with Maurras, but he died advising his friends to stop worrying their heads about romanticism and classicism and to think a little more about the difference between good and bad writing. The sad fact is that behind this classicist campaign there is no literature at all.

It unfortunately appears that the same charge can

be brought against humanism. I read the list of contributors to the volume on *Humanism in America:* Norman Foerster, Louis Trenchard More, Irving Babbitt, Paul Elmer More, G. R. Elliott, T. S. Eliot, Frank Jewett Mather, Jr., Alan Reynolds Thompson, Robert Shafer, Henry Hayden Clark, Stanley P. Chase, Gorham B. Munson, Bernard Bandler II, Sherlock Bronson Gass, Richard Lindley Brown. I heartily agree with Professor Babbitt in his opinion that the text, "By their fruits shall ye judge them," is an excellent touchstone to apply to movements. But there is an overwhelming reason why it cannot be applied in this case. I recognize in the list the name of only one creator, T. S. Eliot, and he, in spite of his genius, has long ceased to create on any important plane. For these we are to exchange Proust, Joyce, Lawrence, Aldous Huxley, Virginia Woolf. Forgive me, but I have not enough of the gambler in me to dare such a transaction, and seek association with what looks so remarkably like a league of the noncreative against the creative.